a guide to
psychotherapy

Gerald Amada, Ph.D.

M. EVANS
Lanham • New York • Boulder • Toronto • Plymouth, UK

Published by M. Evans
An imprint of The Rowman & Littlefield Publishing Group, Inc.
4501 Forbes Boulevard, Suite 200, Lanham, Maryland 20706
http://www.rlpgtrade.com

Estover Road, Plymouth PL6 7PY, United Kingdom

Distributed by National Book Network

British Library Cataloguing in Publication Information Available

Library of Congress Cataloging-in-Publication Data Available

Amada, Gerald.
  A guide to psychotherapy / Gerald Amada.
    p. cm.
  ISBN 978-1-59077-135-8 (pbk. : alk. paper) —
  ISBN 978-1-59077-187-7 (electronic)
  1. Psychotherapy. 2. Psychotherapists. I. Title.
  RC480.A48 2011
  616.89'14—dc22
                                        2010032395

Printed in the United States of America

To my patients
and the students of
City College of San Francisco

We rejected most emphatically the view that we should convert into our own property the patient who puts himself into our hands in seek of help, should carve his destiny for him, force our own ideals upon him, and with the arrogance of a Creator form him in our own image and see that it was good. . . . I would say that after all this is only tyranny, even though disguised by the most honourable motives.

—Sigmund Freud

contents

foreword

My initial excitement over this little gem was with its use as a guide—a Fodor's of the Phrenum! a Marco Polo of the Mind! a Baedekker's of the Brain! Dr. Amada has given us an honest and thorough introduction to the journey of psychotherapy. He whets our interest, he displays the attractions, he allays our psychic xenophobia of a landscape dotted with strange species and snares, but also one laden with great riches. One could not want a more considerate and understanding tour guide.

Dr. Amada offers us not only a fine map and companion for a journey, he affords us full disclosure and the information needed to make independent consumer choices. The marketplace of the mind has long lacked this charting. Potential consumers of therapy services now have the tools for understanding and for responsible and wise decisions.

But this little manual is deceptively simple. Dr. Amada has shrewdly reversed the trap of iatrogenesis, wherein the healing "solution" furthers or even causes the disease. He not only points out the psychotherapeutic path to health, he immediately involves the reader in creating health. Indeed, he predicates health by inviting the traveler to journey with him. This is not just a graceful exposition of distant lands—it is precisely the first step of the journey, the awakening in the reader of both the exhilarating freedom of self-determination and the healing interdependence of collaboration.

Our guide holds out no promise but the opportunity to create the promise. The respect and compassion that grace his offerings are the qualities of health that he presents to one who would liberate oneself from the tyranny of ghosts. And they are the qualities, woven into his gentle process, that promise both liberation from others' ghosts and the hope of mature human harmony.

Dr. Amada has gone a long way to unlocking some important professional mysteries. This candid demythologizing is both a gift and a challenge to the laity. It should be cherished.

Richard Spohn, Director
California Department of Consumer Affairs
1976–1983

preface

A character in one of George Bernard Shaw's plays wittily remarked that all professions were conspiracies against the laity. Psychotherapy as a profession is sometimes seen in this unhappy light by the general public. Perhaps psychotherapists themselves contribute to this dim view by their occasional reluctance to speak out boldly and intelligibly about the positive results of their work.

The following chapters are my attempt to describe and explain in nontechnical language the workings and potential benefits of the professional practice known as psychotherapy, both from the standpoint of the patient and from the vantage point I have had as a therapist. It is my hope that by this means I can help to destigmatize and demystify a subject that has been surrounded by considerable controversy and mystery.

There are a vast number of worthwhile books that provide psychological guidelines to improving one's self-image and mental health. Most often these "self-help" books provide clues to detecting the sneaky psychological influences, past and present, that tend to undermine psychological well-being. Sometimes readers are also given suggestions and encouragement as to how best to overcome what psychologically ails them.

The person in psychological distress may also consult the many fine psychological works that have been written by psychotherapists mainly for psychotherapists. Although many of these books tend to be rather theoretical and abstract, they can provide valuable information about the nature of the human personality as well as offering assistance in understanding the practice of psychotherapy.

In my practice as a psychotherapist I have spent many hours speaking to lay groups about psychotherapy. I discovered that no matter how dissimilar these groups were from one another, they tended to ask many of the same questions about my work. "What is psychotherapy?" "How do you know when you need a therapist?" "How does one go about selecting a competent therapist?" And so on.

This book is an attempt to answer these and other such questions in a manner that, I hope, will be interesting and useful to the reader. The primary audience for this book are those persons who are either considering entering psychotherapy or those who, although they have already seen a psychotherapist, still feel that many of their questions about the psychotherapy experience remain unanswered. In addition, this book might assist the fledgling psychotherapist whose patients inevitably will ask many of the same questions that I will discuss in these chapters.

There are perhaps as many as two hundred and fifty different psychotherapies currently available to the public. Although I have attempted to find a common ground upon which these diverse therapies rest (if such a thing exists), the reader should have little difficulty in detecting in these pages my strong bias in favor of psychoanalytic psychotherapy.

Since the first publication of this book, I have had the pleasurable opportunity of discussing with some of its readers, lay and professional alike, their varied impressions of its strengths and shortcomings. I am indeed grateful to these readers for generously and candidly sharing their observations with me. A man from Southern California wrote to tell me he was "touched" by the warmth and humanness of my writing style. Fellow psychotherapists frequently have remarked that they appreciated the down-to-earth, dignified presentation of ideas and concepts that sometimes defied ready explanation during the course of their psychotherapy sessions with clients. As a result, they often recommended the book as a navigational guide for clients who expressed curiosity about the principles and guidelines that governed their own psychotherapy experience.

Some commentators, on the other hand, complimented the fact that the book, which they viewed as refreshingly dissimilar from many that adorn the self-help bookshelves, did not set down a long litany of unrealistic recipes, remedies, or homilies for an instantly better life. A few, on the other hand, expressed a bit of frustration over my alleged tendency to complexify and overanalyze "simple" psychological questions. Apparently very few, to my heartfelt satisfaction, were left emotionally and intellectually unchallenged and unaffected by what they had found in these pages. I sincerely hope that you, the next reader, will also be touched and enriched by the vast and promising possibilities described in the following chapters.

I owe a debt of deep gratitude to Donald Cliggett, Ph.D., Joel Saldinger, M.D., and Ms. Mary Riordan, for their many helpful ideas and suggestions pertaining to this book.

Ms. Elizabeth Carnes, former promotion manager of University Press of America, the book's original publisher, deserves special thanks for her generous and sensitive assistance in helping me prepare this book for publication.

I also wish to thank my editor, Rick Rinehart, for his support and assistance in relaunching this book. His many kindnesses in shepherding this book toward publication are deeply appreciated. Special thanks to Jehanne Schweitzer, my production editor, for safely navigating this literary craft through some jagged editorial shoals.

I am extremely indebted to Ms. Amelia Lippi for her unstinting help with the earlier copies of the manuscript and for her many acts of kindness and friendship extended to me over the years we have worked together.

My daughter, Robin, deserves special thanks for typing the final copy of the manuscript and for her skillful proofreading.

I am extremely grateful to the other members of my family, Marcia, Naomi, Laurie, Eric, and sons-in-law Jay, Scott, and Ira, who, with understanding and humor, have helped me to keep my feet on the ground while allowing me occasionally to poke my head into the clouds.

Finally, I want to thank my patients for the unique opportunity and privilege they have afforded me by seeking my help. I wish to assure them that sufficient changes have been made in this book to protect their confidentiality without any basic alteration of the truth.

Before proceeding further, I wish to introduce a caveat to the reader: from chapter to chapter, I have alternately used male and female pronouns to designate both patients and therapists quite arbitrarily and, I hope, equitably, and not too jarringly.

Gerald Amada, Ph.D.
San Rafael, California

1

what is
psychotherapy?

Psychotherapy is an intricate process of interaction between two or more complex personalities. One of those persons (the patient)
seeks help with problems of an emotional nature from
a trained professional who, by establishing a positive, trusting (and trustworthy) relationship with the
patient, will attempt to help him mature and grow.
Psychotherapy can also be seen as a healing process
by which a psychotherapist helps a patient learn about
the "self" that he has perhaps been unconsciously and
unsuspectingly concealing, primarily from himself.

There have been many models and analogies used
to describe the essence of psychotherapy, each deserv-
ing respectful recognition, yet each suffering from
inevitable shortcomings. For example, there is the

medical model that, at least in its classic form, implies that a psychiatric patient is suffering from an "illness" and needs to be "cured" by such medically based techniques and procedures as establishing a diagnosis, treatment plan and prognosis. According to the purists of this model, psychotherapy is based strictly upon certain scientific principles and tenets that, if properly studied and applied by the therapist, would lend a healthy degree of predictability, objectivity and verifiability to the treatment.

On the other hand, the friendship model of psychotherapy suggests that the relationship between a patient and his therapist is nothing more nor less than a form of friendship, albeit an exceptional, and most likely unprecedented kind of friendship.

The artistic model of psychotherapy describes the human interaction that takes place in psychotherapy as quintessentially an art form which is creative, aesthetic and, if mastered, even exquisite.

The educational model of psychotherapy infers that the emotionally troubled individual has learned "bad" habits, attitudes and behavioral patterns that a therapist, largely through remedial educative efforts, will help him to "unlearn."

Each of these models has much to recommend it, but since all models are only approximations of reality, no single model can explain or encompass the many complexities, ambiguities and serendipities that constitute the essence of psychotherapy. So, freely borrowing from some of the above-mentioned models, I will attempt to identify the most essential elements of psychotherapy, i.e., what essentially makes this human endeavor work (or fail).

There is a rather widespread misconception that psychotherapists are nothing more than spongy sounding boards or enigmatic computers who mechanically take in information, process it through their machine-like minds and automatically and unerringly punch out scientific answers. Unfortunately, certain psychotherapists deliberately or inadvertently contribute to this myth by affecting an air of perfection, impersonality, impenetrability, and omniscience. This misconception notwithstanding, psychotherapy is best viewed as fundamentally a *human relationship,* although no ordinary human relationship, to be sure.

Well, if psychotherapy is basically a human relationship, what makes it special or different from other relationships? What is its essence? Let us tackle this elusive and complicated subject by considering those factors that tend to support the proposition that the psychotherapeutic relationship is indeed special and unique among human relationships.

First, psychotherapy is a relationship in which a person who is in emotional pain and conflict shares his deepest personal concerns with someone who genuinely *listens.* The therapist listens in no ordinary way. He listens not only to the content of what his patients tell him, but to their tone of voice, the intonations and idiosyncrasies of their speech; he notes their bodily gestures and mannerisms. And he listens also to the quality of connectedness with which the patient communicates, verbally and non-verbally, with him, the therapist. Furthermore, underlying the therapist's listening posture is his patience and willingness, actual eagerness, to help the patient to speak his mind as fully and as richly as he possibly can.

Another facet of the therapist's listening attitude is that he not only listens to what the patient tells him, tacitly or verbally, but he listens for what the patient means by what he tells him. To borrow the title of a book by Theodore Reik, he listens with a "Third Ear" for clues to understanding the more hidden, unconscious recesses of the patient's personality. In this respect, the listening stance of the therapist can be described as dynamic listening; i.e., he is intently listening for and to the dynamic, unconscious psychological forces that lurk secretly beneath the surface of the human personality.

A short example may illustrate this point. A patient I had seen for about a month would proclaim each week that, given his "silly" psychological problems, I would soon assuredly consider him "incurable" and summarily send him on his way. Since I certainly did not consider his problems "silly" or "incurable," nor had any intention of quitting on this patient, I paid particular attention to the manner in which he expressed himself in this regard. It soon became evident to me that the patient was exhibiting a form of contempt for me and my professional skills by, in effect, thinking that I was either a kind of nincompoop who treated emotionally troubled persons lightly (as having "silly" problems) or, even worse, that I was a ruffian who shooed people out of my office the moment I had any doubts about their "curability." In short, it was clear that the patient was rejecting me and psychotherapy in anticipation that I, like others on whom he had depended, would reject him.

I suggested to the patient that he perhaps feared or expected such mistreatment from me and, therefore, seemed to be preparing himself to leave before he was "fired." I also remarked that his problems certainly did not seem silly or insoluble to me. The patient vehemently denied that he had thoughts of leaving therapy and reaffirmed his determination to proceed with the treatment. After a few more sessions he called to notify me that he was terminating therapy, ostensibly because of certain job commitments.

When the patient resumed therapy about one year later he acknowledged that his fears of being rejected by me had caused him to end his therapy. At that time he had sensed overwhelming fears of rejection, but found it impossible to accept my interpretations of his actions. He gradually was able to face and overcome many of his fears about me and, as a result, his other relationships improved appreciably. This illustrates the way in which a therapist listens not only to what is being said, but to what his patients mean by what they say.

A second factor that distinguishes the psychotherapeutic relationship from most other relationships is the non-judgmental attitude of the therapist. During the course of therapy a patient will describe his many interactions with others. Inevitably, there will be times when the patient, like most other people, will behave in an insensitive, humiliating and even cruel manner. Certainly it is not the job of a psychotherapist to condone or countenance such behavior. On the other hand, a therapist realizes that cruel attitudes and behavior are the universal signs of human unhappiness and that merely disliking, criticizing and rebuking a patient for his cruelty or foolishness will only exacerbate his basic conflicts and, therefore, worsen his antisocial behavior.

Although he may at times strongly dislike the way in which a patient behaves, the therapist's unique training, objectivity and self-discipline enable him to refrain from forming and issuing moralistic judgments of him. Rather, the therapist intensely wants to understand and *wants his patient to understand* how and why he sometimes behaves irresponsibly or cruelly. This does not mean, of course, that psychotherapists are devoid of moral values or that they are oblivious to the moral implications and consequences of their patients' behavior. It does mean, however, that a therapist realizes that a censuring and pontificating attitude toward his patients' behavior will only demean and alienate them. Since cruel and insensitive behavior ordinarily stems from feelings of alienation and humiliation in the first place, the therapist attempts to understand and empathize with the anguish that drives a person to acts of inhumanity. The therapist hopes that, by demonstrating his own humanity through non-judgmental acts of understanding and empathy, he will enlist the patient in an earnest attempt to reflect upon and resolve his harmful or destructive tendencies. For it is only by this means that a person can relinquish his tendencies toward irrational or irresponsible behavior.

Another, although intangible, aspect of psychotherapy which tends to distinguish it from other relationships is the deep interest, curiosity and seriousness with which both patient and therapist approach the former's life. In psychotherapy an attitude prevails that the patient and his life are worthwhile, precious and definitely worth knowing about, intimately and purposefully. Whatever the patient thinks and feels, no matter how seemingly trivial, trite or ludicrous, is treated with respect, concern and seriousness. Often, for example, a patient will discover that a fleeting thought, a "bizarre" idea or a momentary instinctual urge, if explored seriously and painstakingly, will lead to penetrating insights about how his mind works and how he lives his life.

For this reason, the therapist strives to know virtually everything about what the patient thinks, feels and does. Obviously, the quest to know everything about another person never meets with complete success. Contrary to popular myth, the patient *always* knows more about what he himself thinks, feels and does than the therapist. Therefore, the therapist is in a catch-up position in relation to the patient; that is, he knows about the patient only what the patient tells about himself.

The therapist realizes that it is his responsibility to help the patient share with him what he knows about himself to whatever extent he can. It has been suggested by one noted authority on this subject that even a patient who spends many years in psychoanalysis will be known to his analyst only as well as a globe-traveling explorer "knows" an entire continent after having set foot just on its tip.

Although this analogy probably has considerable merit, the fact that a therapist always knows far less about a patient than the patient knows about himself need not be a cause for mutual alarm or nihilism. Actually, it is this personal knowledge imbalance between patient and therapist that provides the primary impetus for the growth and development of the therapeutic relationship. The therapist wants to know the patient intimately and, therefore, sets out to induce him to explain himself as best he can. The process of discovering who this person, the patient, really is—inside and outside—can be, like most first discoveries, illuminating and uplifting for patient and therapist alike. For the therapist, being given the opportunity to see the world through the eyes of another person can be a unique privilege and adventure. For the patient, the realization that someone else, an objective and empathic professional, is deeply interested in all aspects of his life and welfare can be a highly moving and deeply cherishable experience.

Finally, I think the psychotherapeutic relationship can be distinguished from most other relationships by the fact that there are relatively few expectations placed upon the patient in psychotherapy. In most relationships mutual expectations play an instrumental role in galvanizing and cementing the ties of the persons involved. For example, in the parent-child relationship, a teenager's allowance or curfew hour may be markedly affected by how well he meets his parents' expectations for carrying out household responsibilities. In the employer-employee relationship, a wage earner's upward (or downward) mobility in a corporation will be greatly determined by how well he meets his supervisors' expectations for productivity, loyalty, punctuality, etc. In the teacher-student relationship, a student's grade point average will definitely be affected by how successfully he meets his teachers' expectations for academic excellence.

Throughout our entire lives—from the time we first finished all of our Pablum or defecated in the toilet (instead of in our diapers) in order to hear our mommies say, "What a wonderful baby you are!"—we have directed much of our emotional energy toward pleasing and fulfilling the expectations of other people. Because mutual expectations play such a natural and integral role in all interpersonal relationships, it is awfully difficult for most people to decide to what extent their strivings and goals are truly self-directed and self-fulfilling, or to what degree they are the ill-begotten concoctions of someone else's thinking and beliefs. For all of us, making such crucial distinctions is a lifelong task, and our success in carrying out this particular task will deeply affect our personal well-being.

Since usually so much of a person's life is pervaded by the expectations of others, most psychotherapy patients naturally anticipate that the therapist will also have definable expectations of them. Consequently, they may behave in ways that they believe are acceptable or desirable to the therapist. For example, if a patient believes that the therapist wants to be amused by him, he may, consciously or not, plan to be especially witty or entertaining in the therapy.

If, however, the therapist does his job well, he will impose few, if any, conditions or expectations upon the patient with respect to the patient's actions and attitudes. In other words, the patient is entirely free to feel, think and express literally anything in therapy, without in any sense trespassing upon a moral or social standard of the therapist. (I have deliberately omitted stating that the patient is free to *behave* as he wishes in therapy, since there are exceptional circumstances—

such as the obviously provocative patient who decides to sip his booze during the therapy session—that may require the therapist to insist upon minimal behavioral conformity to his wishes.)

I am not suggesting that therapists do not have personal expectations of themselves and others. Therapists, like the rest of the human race, certainly have social and moral expectations of other people; however, a therapist's training and expertise enable him to suspend his personal expectations and needs, whatever they may be, when he is helping his patients. In other words, he deliberately and consciously abstains from allowing his own personal expectations to interfere with or eclipse his patients' expectations of themselves.

Thus, the therapist respects the patient's right to feel depressed or elated (or anything in between), to progress, to stand still or to retrogress psychologically and, when the patient is ready, to advance at his own pace, in whatever direction he chooses. The patient is accepted, without qualification or condition, for who he is and does not have to earn the therapist's respect or esteem by improving his attitudes or behavior. Viewed from this perspective, the psychotherapy relationship is easily and positively distinguishable from most other human relationships.

Incidentally, many psychotherapy patients do not regard the non-expectations of the therapist as an unequivocal blessing, at least not at first. Many persons, particularly those with authoritarian or autocratic family backgrounds, feel most secure in relationships that allow or require them to be submissive and acquiescent. Such individuals may feel especially comfortable only when being controlled and piloted by others, even though they will in all likelihood also resent being under someone else's control. Consequently, the social and psychological freedom accorded to the overly conforming patient by the therapist may throw him off guard for a while, even causing him to think that the therapist has an ulterior motive in refusing to control his personal decisions and feelings.

This incredulousness sometimes leads the patient to test the therapist by asking him for advice and/or permission for carrying out his personal decisions. By this means the patient attempts—to use the phrase made famous by Eric Fromm—to "escape from freedom."

Although the freedom to think, feel and be whatever he wants may disconcert or puzzle a patient, most psychotherapy patients eventually come to cherish and appreciate this unique freedom. For many persons, it is precisely this freedom offered by psychotherapy that liberates them from the psychological shackles of their pasts and thereby makes the experience of psychotherapy unique.

2

a brief history
of psychotherapy

Since all societies generate a degree of conflict and unhappiness, the need for what we now call "therapy" has apparently existed since people first became social beings. In response to this need, the earliest societies produced philosophers, priests and shamans, whose primary functions were to grapple with the complexities and dilemmas of human life. Thus, the contemporary psychotherapist may be regarded as the rightful heir to the class of sages and priests who lived many centuries ago.

The diverse psychotherapies of today continue to reflect in varying degrees the thinking, both shamanistic (the healing of illness achieved through the powers of a doctor) and philosophical (explanations of the

individual's problems of adjustment to society), of their
early forebears.

The beginnings of modern psychotherapy are often
traced to Anton Mesmer (1734–1815), an Austrian who
discovered hypnosis, which he used as a method for
treating hysterical conditions. Mesmer became the
center of a cult for a number of years, and although
he himself eventually faded from popularity, hypnosis
regained respectability in the late nineteenth century
largely as a result of the work of Jean-Martin Charcot
(1825–1893). Charcot treated patients with hypnosis for
such conditions as hysterical blindness, seizures, faint-
ing spells and other such disorders, which were evidently prevalent in the nineteenth century.

Unquestionably, the person who is generally
acknowledged as the principal founder of modern psychotherapy is Sigmund Freud (1856–1939). Freud studied with Charcot and although he displayed an early
interest in the workings of hypnosis, his later studies
extended far beyond this field. Freud, as the founder of
psychoanalysis, developed the concept of the unconscious that, until the time of his discovery, was relatively unknown to the field of psychology. Freud's
discovery provided Western culture with a new set of
insights and methods for exploring and understanding
the unconscious and irrational elements of the human
personality.

Psychoanalysis historically has stressed several factors: infantile sexuality, drives, the role of the uncon-

scious, resistances—i.e., obstacles to uncovering unconscious material—and transference. Transference, one of the central concepts of psychoanalysis, refers to the reviving of one's past in the psychotherapy situation. Despite the controversies and rancor that have often surrounded his life and his theories, most psychotherapists who are psychodynamically oriented owe Freud a considerable debt, as witness the countless times he continues to be quoted in the professional discussions and literature of contemporary psychotherapists.

One of the prominent therapists influenced by Freud was Carl Jung (1875–1961), who, in his own writings, downplayed the importance of infantile sexuality. Jung viewed the unconscious as an inheritable, "collective" repository of memories and archetypes—i.e., central themes such as the Great Mother—that originated in the minds of our earliest ancestors.

Alfred Adler (1870–1937), another contemporary of Freud's, minimized the role of the unconscious and sexuality, while tending to stress social factors, such as the need for power, domination and self-esteem.

Other important figures in the psychoanalytic movement, whose impact has been especially felt here in the United States, are Karen Homey (1885–1952), Harry Stack Sullivan (1892–1949), Otto Rank (1884–1939), and Eric Fromm (1900–1980). Those prominent "Neo-Freudian" figures were influential in highlighting the crucial impact of social and interpersonal forces upon the development of the human personality.

Another therapist who gained prominence within the psychoanalytic movement was Wilhelm Reich (1897–1957). In a departure from Freud and psychoanalysis, Reich stressed the biological origins of mental illness. He claimed to have discovered a form of life energy that he treated with orgone therapy and, after modifying this treatment somewhat, bioenergetic therapy.

Fritz Perls (1893–1970), heavily influenced by Reich, was a charismatic figure who, after a period of being attracted to psychoanalysis, stressed the importance of non-verbal, bodily or organismic movement and sensations, which he placed on a par with the mind and mental processes. Perls placed more value on feeling and less on thinking. He also stressed the importance of living in the present and downplayed the importance of reflecting upon one's personal history.

In the United States, an influential school of therapy was developed by Carl Rogers (1902–1987). Based upon a profound belief in the goodness of man, Rogers advocates a therapy which makes a wholehearted attempt, largely by mirroring the clients' statements about their feelings, to arouse and bring forth what is whole, positive and good in the client. Rogers minimizes repressed unconscious factors and stresses the invaluable benefits to be derived from a therapeutic relationship in which the client is treated by the therapist with esteem and "unconditional positive regard." The therapist's optimistic regard for the client will result in a process that will help him grow, mature and socialize with fulfillment.

Consistent with the optimistic trend in American psychotherapy is another approach, transactional analysis, a therapy founded by Eric Berne (1910–1970). Berne's TA seems to have evolved from Adlerian therapy inasmuch as it emphasizes the need to overcome feelings of insecurity and inferiority.

In *Games People Play,* Berne popularized psychological phenomena (such as insincere or domineering behavior) by grouping them into readily understandable and digestible categories known as "games."

According to Berne, each individual responds to his environment by entering one of three ego states (the Parent, Adult or Child). The Parent, an undesirable state, represents harsh and unreasonable morality. The Child, also an objectionable state, is largely equivalent to Freud's concept of the id; i.e., it is the state that results from being overwhelmed by instinctual drives and impulses. The Adult—the more or less ideal state—represents rational and mature morality that, if maintained, can control and civilize the Child and temper the Parent. Thomas Harris (1910–1995), author of the 1970s best seller, *I'm O.K.—You're O.K.,* utilizes these concepts to point the way toward achieving a state of psychological well-being or "OKness."

A school of therapy that stands in sharp contrast to psychoanalysis is behavioral therapy. This form of therapy is often associated with Joseph Wolpe (1915–1997), who created the technique known as systematic desensitization. This technique entails helping the patient overcome a particular symptom (e.g., a fear of heights) by taking measured and manageable steps up a hierarchy of dangerous situations until the target symptom is conquered.

Clearly, the focus of attention in behavior therapy is upon observable and objectively evaluated behavior. The behavior therapist identifies the manifest and undesirable symptom, such as a phobia, and then applies a set of directives aimed at modifying or "extinguishing" the symptom. This procedure is heavily based upon the early work of B. F. Skinner (1904–1990), the founder of behavior therapy, who developed the method known as operant conditioning. A patient who has developed undesirable behavior is conditioned to rid himself of it by being presented with a set of rewards, which reinforce his healthier behavior, and punishments, which eliminate his maladaptive behavior.

An adjunctive technique in behavior therapy is progressive relaxation, which involves breathing exercises undertaken while imagining pleasant scenes. The clear and explicit goal is to reduce anxiety, and to replace it by a state of calm and tranquility.

In recent years the existential school of psychotherapy has gained considerable recognition and respect. Championed principally by Rollo May (1909–1994) in this country, existential therapy emphasizes the immediacy of existence. Within the human condition is an abyss of meaninglessness and incompleteness. In existential therapy, the therapist and patient directly confront this abyss by entering into a highly personal and equal partnership characterized by mutual regard and compassion. May's challenge to the horrific and imperfect in human existence once prompted him to describe his form of therapy in the following epigrammatic manner: "I'm not O.K., you're not O.K. and that's O.K."

A relative latecomer to the array of psychotherapeutic treatments made available to the public in this country is primal therapy. The founder of primal therapy, Arthur Janov (b. 1924), received wide acclaim following publication of his book, *The Primal Scream.* In Janov's theory the psychotherapy patient has been devastated by an event of early childhood known as the primal trauma. This trauma is brought on by an awareness that the child's parents do not love him. According to Janov, the child undergoes a "primal scene" early in life in which he realizes there is no hope of being loved for what he is.

In response to his primal pain the child develops psychological defenses which lead to a neurosis. Primal therapy sets out to rid the patient of his neurosis by placing him in a relatively isolated living situation for a prolonged period (usually several weeks) with instructions to abstain from drugs and other tension-reducing diversions. The patient meets only with his therapist each day in open-ended sessions. The specific goal of these sessions is to induce the patient to express his deepest feeling toward his parents. Since these emotions have by now reached volcanic proportions, the patient expresses them through primal screams. After completing this intensive phase of the treatment, the patient returns for perhaps another six months of therapy in a primal group. Janov assumes that by this time and by this means the post-primal person will have returned to his unneurotic or "real" self.

Since there are perhaps as many as two hundred fifty different therapies in use today, it is obviously not possible to cover each one thoroughly in this book. Such therapies as feminist therapy, family therapy, sex therapy, radical therapy, reality therapy, and rational-emotive therapy have proliferated in recent years. And many more are sure to follow. For a more detailed and comprehensive explanation of the particular schools of therapy, the reader is encouraged to consult the writings of the practitioners and advocates of the diverse treatments.

3

who are the people providing psychotherapy?

In the United States psychotherapists currently include approximately 100,000 clinical social workers, 50,000 psychiatrists, 90,000 clinical psychologists, 20,000 psychiatric nurses, and 100,000 counselors.

Clinical social workers have received a Master's degree from an accredited graduate school of social work. Their graduate education includes such courses as human growth and behavior, social work administration, casework, group work, and community organization. Social work graduate school normally lasts two years, during which time the student spends two or three days a week acquiring practical experience by working in a "field placement," that is, in a social work agency. In addition to, or as part of, their clinical skills, social workers are apt to be especially conversant with and effective in utilizing social support systems, organizations and groups (such as recreation and welfare agencies) in meeting their clients' psychological needs. Psychiatrists are medical doctors who commonly have completed a one-year general internship and three to five years in psychiatric residency, more than likely in affiliation with a hospital. Since psychiatrists are physicians, they are particularly adept at assessing a person's need for psychotropic medications. Their medical training enables psychiatrists to be particularly knowledgeable in the treatment of psychosomatic illness (physical illness caused by emotional stress). Although the medical model within which psychiatrists work has been much maligned by some nonmedical therapists, many psychiatrists attribute the organized and disciplined quality of their professional work to the unique rigor of the medical training they have received.

In order to be legally designated a clinical psychologist it is usually necessary to have a Ph.D. in clinical psychology from an accredited graduate school. To receive this degree ordinarily requires four or more years of graduate school, including the completion of a dissertation. The clinical psychology program typically includes courses in psychological testing and assessment, abnormal psychology, psychopathology, child development, and the development of the human personality. For most of their graduate years clinical psychology students undertake a course of field work experience that entails working two or three days a week in a clinical setting such as a mental health program. In order to qualify for licensure as a clinical psychologist many states require two years of full-time post-doctoral experience in a psychiatric facility. Psychologists are particularly qualified to provide psychological testing and assessment services and to design and carry out psychological research. Their psychotherapeutic skills are generally enhanced by the systematic and exacting quality of their educational training.

Psychiatric nurses have received a Master's degree from a psychiatric nursing program of an accredited graduate school. Usually an enrollment of at least two years is required to complete this course of study. Psychiatric nursing programs offer such courses as psychiatric theory, child and adult development, and family and group dynamics. The psychiatric nurse is especially proficient in evaluating the effect of a person's physical environment and physical functioning upon her mental health.

The 100,000 licensed counselors previously mentioned are made up of individuals from several professional disciplines and backgrounds. Among these disciplines are counseling, counseling psychology, rehabilitation counseling, educational counseling, and marriage and family counseling. Practically all of these counselors have received at least a Master's degree in their respective fields.

The aforementioned psychotherapists—clinical social workers, psychiatrists, clinical psychologists,

psychiatric nurses, and counselors—have each undergone an intensive process of supervision and review
in order to qualify for the state-conferred license that
enables them legally to practice psychotherapy.

In most states, however, psychiatrists are licensed
to practice medicine, rather than to practice only the
medical specialty of psychiatry. Psychiatrists may then
receive eligibility or certification to practice their specialty from national voluntary professional associations
and boards. However, they may work as psychiatrists
without this eligibility or certification. Most states
require that a prospective psychotherapist undergo
several years of clinical supervision provided by a state-
licensed psychotherapist. (The state-licensed supervisor
is usually a member of the aspirant's professional discipline, but she may represent a kindred discipline, as in
the case of a psychologist supervising a social worker,
or vice-versa.) In addition, the prospective psychotherapist must usually surmount the state-required hurdles
of written and oral examinations before qualifying for
her license.

There are a great number of unlicensed persons
who, although they have no special training in psychotherapy or counseling, advertise themselves as healers
and counselors, evidently hoping that no one will ask
to see their credentials.

Which therapist a patient chooses—psychologist,
social worker, psychiatrist, nurse, or counselor—is very
much an individual matter. It is generally recognized

that these professional disciplines have a great deal in common with each other. Insofar as the psychotherapy patient is concerned, unless she is receiving medications as part of her treatment, she will probably find it difficult to distinguish how one discipline differs from another in the practice of psychotherapy.

4

when should
i enter
psychotherapy?

The decision to enter psychotherapy may be based upon a wide range of considerations and dissatisfactions. For some people the dissatisfactions may rear their nasty heads in the social sphere. Extreme interpersonal shyness, anxiety, awkwardness, suspiciousness and overconformity may serve to undermine a person's ability to form and sustain rewarding social relationships and thereby deepen his sense of isolation and loneliness.

Many persons are confounded by their own behavior. They repeatedly form self-destructive relationships, say and do things which are inimical to their own interests, and generally cannot anticipate the consequences of their own actions. Despite profound desires to form affectionate attachments, they unwittingly alienate their friends and acquaintances. Sometimes the overweening need to dominate and control relationships sabotages the opportunity for interpersonal fulfillment. Others are chronically beset by physical symptoms that have their roots in emotional stress and conflict (often referred to as psychosomatic symptoms). The physical manifestations of emotional stress are varied and sometimes become quite debilitating. They may include headaches, constipation, overeating, undereating, sleeplessness, fatigue, ulcers, and many other physical disorders. Although many or all of these symptoms may be caused by physiological or neurological factors, many persons who suffer from them actually receive a clean bill of health from their physicians because sophisticated medical tests reveal no physical impairment. Such medical findings strongly suggest that the patient's physical symptoms are "proclamations" from his body that something is awry psychologically.

For some persons the breakdown of rationality and self-control causes the meteoric eruption of instinctual drives and impulses. When this happens a person may be prone to temper tantrums, obsessions, compulsions, nightmares and even violent behavior.

There are other, perhaps more vague, personal difficulties which sometimes propel a person toward considering psychotherapy. A decided lack of concentration, direction and motivation, academic underachievement, acute or recurrent depression, nagging suicidal thoughts, chronic struggles in gaining and maintaining employment, and a generalized sense of low self-esteem are legitimate causes for concern. Of course there are even more serious and acute problems which plague vast numbers of people, such as crippling phobias, drug abuse, an intense sense of doom, an unalterable belief that one is about to fall apart or break down, and finally, a consistent and fixed conviction of being universally hated and even persecuted (often referred to as paranoia).

The question, inevitably, is, "Since most people are affected, to an extent, by at least one of the psychological concerns mentioned, does that mean that everyone is in need of psychotherapy?" Obviously not. Many people resolve their personal conflicts through the gratifications they derive from love relationships, friendships, recreation and athletics, artistic pursuits, affiliations with religious, social or political organizations, and, if they are very fortunate, through creative occupational activity. If personal problems can be resolved by means of these potentially gratifying outlets, why bother undertaking psychotherapy?

Because, for certain people, at certain important times in their lives, these outlets do not sufficiently address or resolve immediate and central conflicts. For example, a woman who is married to a knavish and sadistic husband seriously contemplates divorce. Because she is torn between contradictory feelings of loyalty, security and attachment on the one hand, and feelings of entrapment, resentment and desperation on the other, she turns to her friends for advice and support. Most of her friends advise her to leave the "son of a bitch" immediately and permanently, although a few may counsel a more cautious approach. Perhaps one or two friends may even suggest that the beatings she receives are her inevitable and inescapable lot in life and that she should willingly accept the destructive nature of her marital relationship. She is naturally confused by the diverse and conflicting opinions she receives. She understandably suspects some of her friends of being emotionally involved in her conflicts and, therefore, quite subjective in their viewpoints and encouragements. The flood of advice and prodding creates great anxiety and immobilizes her.

Feeling helpless, she begins to take Valium whenever her upsets become too intense. This means of escape becomes habit-forming and insidious. At the suggestion of a friendly neighbor she takes up jogging, and although this activity vastly improves her physical health, she continues to agonize over her marriage. She then tries immersing herself in television soap operas, learns to play the violin fairly well and joins a bridge club. Although these social outlets offer intellectual stimulation, social contacts and a good degree of consolation and support, the nagging and unresolved problems of her marriage will simply not go away. After mistakenly thinking that she has exhausted all possible sources of help, she begins to despair, becomes increasingly depressed and perhaps contemplates suicide.

This hypothetical, but all too familiar vignette provides a useful, although admittedly rather general answer to our original question—how does one determine whether one should enter psychotherapy? First, psychological conflict, anxiety or depression has reached beyond the threshold which the person normally finds tolerable and there is a marked interference with or deterioration of the ordinary means of coping with the demands of everyday life. Second, as occurred in our hypothetical case, other remedial means of resolving emotional conflicts—social, athletic, artistic, etc.—have been considered and explored with insufficient success.

An additional reason a person may want to consider entering psychotherapy involves the frightening and disintegrative nature of the psychological conflicts which remain unresolved. If significant emotional conflicts are not resolved a person can be sorely burdened with pain. This emotional pain can eventually cause one to feel that he carries within himself an unexorcised "evil" or badness. Since he cannot get to the bottom of why he feels so miserable, he irrationally attributes his suffering to imaginary malevolent and detestable qualities within himself. This of course further corrodes his sense of self.

When Dorothy discovered who the Wizard of Oz really was, she no longer felt awe and fear of him. Similarly, a person who fears his inner conflicts will find that, by learning about the unconscious forces that are active within himself, he has little of which to be realistically afraid. Such a discovery is achieved through the process of psychotherapy.

5

how should i select
a psychotherapist?

To begin by approaching matters from a cautionary standpoint, there are several types of psychotherapists who are not qualified to provide psychotherapy. One such therapist is a relative, friend or social acquaintance of the prospective patient, even if any of these is an otherwise highly qualified therapist.

In order for psychotherapy to be effective and useful to the client he must feel that the therapeutic relationship is safe, protected and confidential. He needs to be assured that no information regarding his psychotherapy, including the very fact that he sees a psychotherapist, will be communicated purposely or inadvertently to friends, relatives, co-workers, etc., unless he himself willingly decides to transmit the

---

information. (This fundamental condition must often be violated in the case of court-referred or child clients, both of whom usually require consultation with others significant to the client, such as probation officers, parents and teachers). Furthermore, the client should be assured that the therapist is a competent and objective professional who has no vested interest in how and when he resolves his problems.

A friend or relative who "doubles" as a therapist unavoidably contaminates the therapeutic relationship because he obviously cannot assure his friend-patient anonymity and confidentiality. The essential pact of privacy on the part of the therapist will likely lead to considerable mutual discomfort and tension between the friend-patient and friend-therapist throughout their social encounters. Unconsciously motivated "slips" and revelations on the part of either the patient or therapist will quickly erode the confidential nature of the relationship. This erosion can turn a festive social gathering into a social disaster and, consequently, lamentably destroy all prospects of future therapeutic progress.

It is also unrealistic for a prospective patient to expect that a friend or relative, even one who happens to be a magnificent therapist, will be prepared fully to divest himself of his personal investment in him and his problems. This friend or relative will naturally consider how his patient's problems and their resolution will affect him *personally* since their relationship is basically personal and nothing he attempts to do professionally will change that fact. The friend-therapist will understandably want to know, for example, whether the resolution of his friend-patient's problems will adversely affect him. Let's say the friend-patient decided that a new job offer to work in Singapore for five years is an ideal opportunity to overcome his present woes. To what extent can a friend-therapist transcend his personal regret over giving up this friendship for five years in order to extend to his friend heartfelt and vital endorsement of his decision? Incidentally, a psychotherapist who has no "personal" tie to his patient may, for various reasons, have similar feelings about his patient's planned sojourn in Singapore; however, he is less likely, due to his training, to allow his regrets to color and control his therapeutic attitude. Good friendships are to be safeguarded and cherished, but converting a friend into your therapist will probably leave you with less of a friend and not much of a therapist.

Another kind of "therapist" to avoid is someone who purports to be a psychotherapist but is not properly trained, accredited or licensed in the field of mental health or psychotherapy. Certainly, even excellent psychotherapy training and officially recognized credentials do not guarantee that a therapist will demonstrate skill and competency. On the other hand, a lack of requisite training on the part of a practitioner of "psychotherapy" will almost assuredly *guarantee* that a client will be treated incompetently and unprofessionally. A professionally untrained and uncredentialed person who poses as a psychotherapist is very likely, due to his lack of essential training, to be overinvolved and overidentified with his clients, thereby making it too difficult for him to maintain an objective view of their problems.

A third type of therapist on whom a "Beware" sign might be placed is the person who offers his clients such messianic blandishments as simple, immediate cures and unbounded happiness; in some cases, all in one exhilarating weekend. Human personalities are highly complex. Therefore, human conflicts and problems have a high degree of complexity. Coping with our own internal stresses (drives, dreams, physical discomforts, etc.,) is usually a quite demanding task in itself. When we add to this task the normal pressures of dealing with family, love relationships, our job, school, finances and so on, we quickly realize that conflicts are an intrinsic part of our daily existence and that they will never go away completely. True, most severe emotional conflicts can certainly be appreciably alleviated and more effectively resolved as one develops increased self-esteem and awareness. However, a therapist who implies or promises a virtual end to all human worries and struggles is probably either a charlatan or a grandiose eccentric.

Let us now take a more positive step toward seeking a qualified and competent therapist. How do you start?

Many people devote little forethought and inquiry to finding a therapist. Many of these same people will spend weeks, even months, anguishing and ruminating over which car they will purchase. They test-drive twenty cars, consult *Consumer Report,* discuss the matter with anyone who will listen to their plight and finally make what they hope is an intelligent choice. But when they experience a psychological crisis they unthinkingly open the Yellow Pages, read the listing of therapists and select, for instance, a therapist whose name is similar to that of their once favorite nursery school teacher. Perhaps without asking the therapist a single thing about his professional background, training and qualifications, they immediately request an appointment and, fingers anxiously crossed, hope for the best.

Having a good car may indeed be a matter of life or death, but is selecting a therapist—a professional person to help you with your most intimate and central concerns—really a matter of such little importance as to be approached by a trial-and-error, "let-your-fingers-do-the-walking," procedure? If you wish to perform at least as well as your new car, you owe it to yourself to be reasonably thorough and selective in choosing your new therapist.

How can one be thorough and selective in his choice of a therapist? There are several useful methods for selecting a therapist, none of which, admittedly, is foolproof (I will soon explain the pitfalls). Many public and institutional (e.g., hospital) libraries have registries which contain listings of licensed and credentialed psychotherapists: psychologists, social workers, marriage and family counselors, nurses and psychiatrists. These registries may give some clue to the professional training and qualifications of the prospective therapist by indicating the educational institutions he attended and is presently affiliated with, articles and/or books he has published, and perhaps his previous professional assignments and achievements. If this bit of investigation is unilluminating or confusing, it may then be helpful to call the local Mental Health Association or chapter of professional psychotherapists in order to request recommendations from those organizations. Since an informal network of mental health professionals exists in nearly every community, the prospective patient can perhaps receive his most reliable referral from a mental health professional whom he already knows and trusts. If this is not possible, his physician may provide him with a dependable referral.

The minimum fee for private therapy is usually between thirty and thirty-five dollars. There seems to be no maximum fee, and since therapists, like others who provide important commodities, tend to charge what the traffic will bear, fees for the well-to-do may reach as high as one hundred dollars an hour and more. The majority of private therapists of my own acquaintance charge between fifty and ninety dollars per hourly session. There is no necessary correlation between the amount of money spent for therapy and the quality of treatment received.

If one cannot afford private fees, he will probably be eligible for the psychological services of a public facility which usually sets fees on a manageable, sliding-scale basis. The potential drawbacks of using public facilities are waiting periods, less choice over who provides the therapy and for how long, and the tendency of public clinics to assign relatively inexperienced therapists who turn over rather rapidly. Nevertheless, some public clinics provide excellent therapeutic services, despite their traditional problems in making ends meet.

Assuming that several psychotherapists have been recommended to him, the prospective client may decide to call each in succession or he may elect to call only one. When he calls, it might be well to briefly explain (without too much historical detail) the reason he has for seeking psychotherapy and to elicit from the therapist such essential information as: (a) the particular clinical services he provides (e.g., hypnosis, individual therapy, group therapy, couple counseling, etc.), (b) the theoretical orientation of the therapist (e.g., psychoanalytic, gestalt, behavioral, Jungian, etc.), (c) the current availability of the therapist, and (d) his fees, including whether his services are covered by existing insurance or government programs. If he is satisfied with the impressions he has received from the call, he may wish to schedule an initial evaluative session.

The prospective client may prefer to bypass all this rigmarole by receiving a referral from a friend or relative who has, through his own psychotherapy experiences, reliable information regarding qualified psychotherapists. There are some contraindications to the arrangement whereby close friends receive psychotherapy from the same therapist (such as the tendency of friends to compete sometimes needlessly for the favoritism of their shared therapist). A competent psychotherapist will be aware of these contraindications and will most likely initiate discussion of them with the patient. The patient should not be too surprised if the therapist advises against his seeing the same therapist his friend sees.

As mentioned earlier, these procedures for finding a qualified and competent therapist are not foolproof; they do have certain inherent drawbacks. For example, despite glowing recommendations and an impressive professional reputation, a given psychotherapist may not be, for personality, ethnic, geographic, economic or other reasons, the most suitable therapist for a particular person. Also, one must take into account the fact that even the best of friends may have widely different perspectives with regard to the kind of person each can trust and find helpful. Thus, Jill's "marvelous" therapist may conceivably turn out to be her best friend Jan's unexpected nemesis.

In order to reduce the possibility of a serious mismatch between therapist and client one might attempt the following course of action. In the initial evaluative session with the therapist, ask for pertinent information regarding her professional training and qualifications. Then attempt to discuss your personal concerns as thoroughly and comprehensively as possible. Before leaving the session, non-defensively request her to do the following: (a) offer you in at least a preliminary manner some explanation or impression of your difficulties, and (b) briefly describe how she intends to work with you.

Without seeking brilliant or highly definitive statements from the therapist, the prospective patient can by this means make an intelligent evaluation of the therapist and thereby arrive at a final decision with a minimum of risk. He of course should keep in mind that this decision, like most personal decisions, is not irrevocable.

6

what's right for me? individual or group psychotherapy?

Since most of this book is written primarily about the workings of individual psychotherapy, I will take time here to delineate some of the features and potentialities of group psychotherapy. Perhaps following this discussion the reader will be better prepared to decide for herself which form of therapy is better suited to her particular needs.

Sometimes the nature of a person's particular set of psychological difficulties may be a strong consideration in whether she selects individual or group psychotherapy. For example, a person's serious drinking problem might be a reasonable cause for her to employ the group therapy services of Alcoholics Anonymous. Those persons who are vexed with problems of overeating and being overweight might very well benefit from the group therapy fare of Weight Watchers. In other words, certain therapy groups offer the assuring feature of bringing together persons troubled by similar types of distressing behavior.

There are numerous and decided advantages to participating in cohesive, intimate groups with others who are undergoing trials much like one's own, among which are the following:

First, many persons who suffer from unremitting emotional conflicts feel that their problems are entirely unique (and, therefore, weird), that no one else in the world experiences such depth and exquisiteness of misery as themselves. Consequently, such persons feel extreme desolation and emptiness in their lives, even when they are in the midst of friendly social relationships. Psychotherapy groups are endowed with marvelous opportunities for isolated and lonely people to overcome their burdensome beliefs that they are the only ones who feel as they do. As group members learn about one another they eventually come to realize that in most respects their emotional tribulations are more universal than singular, that however unhappy they may be, there are others who feel not awfully different from themselves. Group therapy members, by observing and learning about each other, usually come to the realization that they are not as alone or as "strange" as they had first thought.

It is common knowledge that most people respect themselves more and feel better after they have personally assisted someone else. It is also common knowledge that most people as they are growing up are not given sufficient motivation or inducement to expend their emotional energies in serving the welfare of others. Because many people find it so painfully perplexing and difficult to be of service to others, they become deprived of an essential source of self-esteem: their own altruism.

Psychotherapy group members invariably become highly significant to one another, value each other and come to give important parts of themselves through their participation in the group. Group members discover methods for advising, encouraging and supporting each other in ways which accrue to each a sense that she has something worthwhile to impart to someone else and, therefore, she herself is most certainly worthwhile. Surely, the opportunities which are inherent in group therapy for participants to give of themselves are all-important benefits to be gained from this form of treatment.

Since most people in our society are raised in families, it is ordinarily within the family that our emotional growth and our emotional conflicts originate and develop. Group therapy serves as an excellent model or microcosm for the primary family. Usually to a strong degree, group members form relationships with each other which are sibling-like in nature. Thus, rivalries, pettiness, misunderstandings, conflicts, fondness, and alliances develop in a psychotherapy group much as they would in the primary family experience.

At the same time the therapist, as well as certain group members, will be perceived and reacted to as representing parental or authoritative figures.

Since the group therapy process recaptures the patient's earlier family experiences, the patient is psychologically thrust back into her own past, there to reenact and reorganize it. In other words, the emotional conflicts which originally arose between the patient and her parents and siblings will be well replicated in her experience in the therapy group. By reviving old memories and feelings the group therapy experience affords its members the chance to work through and correct the misperceptions and misapprehensions which have long interfered with their interpersonal relationships.

Perhaps a hypothetical example will illuminate this point. A group therapy patient becomes highly anxious each time a conflict takes place between two other patients. She compulsively leaps between the antagonists and poses as peacemaker. This offers her momentary relief, but inevitably she comes to feel exploited, since she realizes that no one really appreciates her presumptuousness and interference. Finally, she is questioned about this annoying proclivity of hers. She admits that she blunders this way in her own personal life and has long and futilely searched for a better means to control her peacekeeping tendencies.

She is astutely questioned by another patient as to whether she was a mediator of sorts when she was a child. The patient ponders the question carefully and then recalls that her parents fought constantly when she was young. In the midst of their quarrels they often threatened divorce. Whenever she heard these threats, the patient panicked and then intervened between her parents, attempting to placate and soothe them. She deeply resented the helpless and humiliating position in which her parents placed her, but felt that without her repeated intercessions the home would break up.

Eventually, the parents did divorce. The patient was left feeling bereft and irrationally blamed herself for the outcome. She convinced herself that if she had only tried harder, if she had said the *right* thing at the *right* time, her parents would have reconciled their differences. Since that time, she has always felt fearful whenever conflicts arose between people she cared about, and, consequently, she could not help insinuating herself into the fray.

At this point one of the group members gently asks the patient, "So, you didn't think the conflict which took place here could be resolved without your help?"

The patient, a bit sheepishly, acknowledges, "I guess not." The group members suggest to the patient that she allow the conflict to resume without interference. The patient grudgingly consents and then, in the here-and-now, observes two group members clash and then constructively resolve their differences. The patient is amazed and greatly pleased with herself for her self-control. She is complimented by other group members for her breakthrough. She has made a significant first step toward overcoming a disturbing personality trait that has persisted since childhood.

It is quite common for a person to grow up in a family that has seriously deficient social aptitudes and, therefore, few social contacts or outlets. Children who are raised in such families often have no positive model that they can emulate in developing social relationships. As a result, they may find it very hard to trust and establish rapport with others. In attempting to form social ties, they often lack the rudiments of social skills, such as how to make small talk, ask evocative questions, respond openly, and so on.

Psychotherapy groups can be extremely effective guides for a person who has a paucity of such skills. Each group member receives ongoing and unvarnished feedback from the group regarding the effect she is having upon others. She learns, sometimes a bit painfully, what pleases and displeases others about herself, what shenanigans and idiosyncrasies of hers "work" and do not work, and she will come to learn what the overused term "communication" really means when one is attempting to form intimate relations with others. In this respect, a therapy group is a masterful teacher of interpersonal competence and versatility.

These potential benefits of group psychotherapy obviously are not exhaustive, but it is hoped they will give the reader a basis of comparison and choice when she considers whether to enter individual or group psychotherapy. In the final analysis, each person must find her own pathways in deciding between individual and group therapy. Some persons give individual therapy a "trial run" and, after acquiring a reasonable foundation of self-understanding by this means, opt for group therapy. The reverse is also true: a person may first enter group therapy and later undergo a course of individual treatment. There are some individuals who undertake both group and individual therapy concurrently with considerable success. The two therapies might be provided by the same therapist or by two different therapists. In any case, each person is different. Some persons benefit far more from individual therapy than group therapy, and vice-versa. Certainly the professional competence and know-how of the therapist one chooses, whether she is a group or individual therapist, will be one of the factors that will strongly determine the amount of benefit one derives from either the individual or group therapy experience.

7

does psychotherapy really work?

Obviously, psychotherapy does not always meet with success. Perhaps an unwavering mismatch between patient and therapist produces a stalemate in the treatment. Or, as often happens, a patient may be more receptive to a different form of therapy than is being offered, as, for example, when a patient decides that the insight-oriented psychoanalytic therapy she receives is too gradual and painstaking and that she will instead try her hand at a behavior modification approach to her problems.

Although psychotherapy, much like the other human endeavors of education, politics and medicine, rarely succeeds perfectly, its rate of failure is not as great as some of its opponents suggest. Occasionally a sensational newspaper story will describe a murder or suicide committed by a psychiatric patient, leaving the ineradicable impression, correct or not, that something went awry in the psychotherapy that caused this person to carry out an irrational and destructive act. To view matters from a very different angle, how newsworthy is a true story that describes how Mrs. Jones overcame her depression, developed a greater liking for herself and received a promotion at the office, all because of the benefits she derived from psychotherapy? With an estimated 40 million Americans receiving some form of psychotherapy today, there are an untold number of Mrs. Joneses whom the public never hears about. The manner in which the public learns from the mass media about psychotherapy can markedly color its opinions about the effectiveness of psychological treatment.

There are many writers who have studied the successes and failures of psychotherapy. Inevitably, some of them have cast serious doubts upon the value and benefits of therapy. One of the most forceful and frequently quoted is the researcher, H. J. Eysenck who, after surveying 8,000 psychotherapy patients in England, concluded that the available data "fail to prove that psychotherapy, Freudian or otherwise, facilitates the recovery of neurotic patients." There are many flaws in Eysenck's study, such as the fact that the groups he studied were not randomly selected and were not comparably "ill." Yet, for reasons that are not altogether clear, this particular study of Eysenck's has gained great credibility among therapy's detractors.

On the other hand, there are many reliable research findings that support the claim that psychotherapy is indeed effective in dealing with psychological stress. For example, W. Follette and N. Cummings in their 1967 study of the pre-paid health plan of Kaiser-Permanente in California found that patients who received psychotherapy were less prone to overutilize medical services than patients who did not undergo psychotherapy. The fact that psychotherapy patients manifested fewer physical symptoms and complaints than their non-psychotherapy counterparts suggests, at least in this instance, that psychotherapy can be quite effective in helping persons with emotional difficulties.

Of course, each year a wide range of articles and books dealing with the successful treatment of psychotherapy patients appears in the psychiatric literature. Much of this literature is highly readable and easily accessible to the general public. Much of it has also been popularized in such reputable magazines as *Psychology Today*.

Economic considerations sometimes play a curious role in determining whether psychotherapy is deemed successful or not. When we purchase most commodities or services, whether they are refrigerators or the carpenter's new door, we have a tangible idea of what such items should cost. We also have certain concrete yardsticks for measuring the quality of the work or commodity purchased. If the carpenter's door falls off the hinges and the refrigerator breaks down in a week, we can quickly and correctly decide that we have not gotten our money's worth.

How can a person apply economic principles to her experience in psychotherapy? If, for instance, she spends thirty dollars a week in psychotherapy, what might she have to give up in order to incur this ongoing expense? If it is an occasional dinner out or a vacation, she must weigh the loss of these psychologically beneficial treats against what she can gain from psychotherapy. Now, how can she do this? How will she evaluate in monetary terms how much increased self-esteem, greater insight, bolstered self-confidence and improved social relationships—the potential rewards of therapy—are worth to her?

For some people, this choice presents a formidable struggle, sometimes resulting in the decision to forfeit therapy. Yet for many others the personal improvements that result from psychotherapy are priceless, despite whatever financial sacrifices therapy sometimes requires. Self-esteem, confidence, insight and self-respect are intangible qualities. Since it is impossible to put a price on or to quantify these personal qualities, it is enormously difficult for most people to determine precisely the level of success they have reached as a result of receiving psychotherapy. They may need to ask themselves many times, "Are the strides I am making due to therapy 'real,' and are they worth the financial sacrifices?"

One additional factor which makes it extremely difficult to determine the exact success of one's psychotherapy is the vagueness of the term "success." The effects of psychotherapy are multidimensional; that is, people can improve in more than one direction at a time. If, for example, a person feels more confident as a result of her therapy, but uses her self-confidence to bully others, can we truly regard her therapy as successful?

A librarian who entered therapy quite depressed was performing her work in a very orderly and efficient manner. She was, therefore, evaluated very highly by her administrative superiors. After undergoing psychotherapy for several months the librarian's depression lifted, but her work became somewhat careless and disorganized in the process. Although she generally began to feel uplifted and spirited, her supervisors thought that her therapy was undermining her, since her work performance had so deteriorated. *They* considered her therapy (which they had themselves encouraged her to undertake) to be a failure, while *she* was convinced that it was an irrefutable success. Which was it?

Psychotherapy has been of immeasurable value to vast numbers of people. Those who are skeptical of this fact might find it helpful and illuminating to speak with acquaintances who have actually had a psychotherapy experience. It is likely that they will in this way receive first-hand and fairly reliable information regarding the benefits to be derived from psychotherapy.

8

will it rob me of
my individuality?

It is quite common for many prospective patients to anticipate that psychotherapy will nullify their originality, initiative and independence; in other words, robotize them. Although one should not automatically rule out the possibility that long-term psychotherapy will produce such adverse results, the dread of losing one's personal individuality and integrity as a result of psychotherapy is usually quite exaggerated and unfounded.

It is interesting and ironic to note that many people who fear that they will relinquish their individuality to a psychotherapist are quite willing, even determined, to give up their independence and identity in an endless number of unhealthy pursuits. For example, a person may diligently avoid a psychotherapist because he fears becoming overly dependent on him and yet heedlessly join a cult in which he will become a completely anonymous cipher. He may perhaps indulge in compulsively hoarding and gorging huge quantities of food to overcome dependency anxieties, rather than talk with a therapist about what ails him. Or, he may readily and repeatedly depend upon his co-workers for advice and understanding even though they are rarely able to offer him the help he needs. Disappointed with the futility of his discussions with co-workers and acquaintances, he may well turn to a habitual use of mind-altering drugs (another form of dependency).

In other words, many of those who are violently allergic to any prospect of forfeiting their individuality to a psychotherapist are quite adept at submerging their sense of identity in such things as drugs, charismatic organizations and unfulfilling relationships.

Why, then, is there such an overriding concern with losing individuality in therapy? In our society one is often taught quite young the "estimable" importance, frequently championed by two badly outworn clichés, of "standing-on-your-own-two-feet" and "pulling-yourself-up-by-your-own-bootstraps." Great pride is taken in the illusion that one can truly mature and thrive without essential help from others. This disdain for dependency in relationships is inculcated early in life, and reinforced in a multitude of ways by parents who also had it drummed into them when they were quite young that "rugged individualism" is essentially good for the character and soul of a person. Conversely, and logically, dependency, particularly dependency upon parents or parental figures (such as psychotherapists), becomes transformed into a huge bugbear.

We must certainly acknowledge that a good degree of self-sufficiency and independence is essential to one's emotional well-being, but the acute fear of depending upon others from which many people suffer very often drives them into a false and frightening "independence" that can lead to loneliness and wretched unhappiness.

To return to the original question: "Can psychotherapy rob a person of his individuality?," most often the reverse is true. After a period of successful psychotherapy most people show signs of increasing self-awareness, originality, spontaneity, decisiveness and emotional autonomy; in other words, the unmistakable hallmarks of genuine self-government and independence. Furthermore, it is helpful for the prospective psychotherapy patient to realize that it is he himself who regulates the psychological impact which the therapist will have upon him. Most persons are sufficiently well equipped with powerful and versatile psychological defense mechanisms as well as deeply ingrained attitudes that enable them to maintain their integrity and selfhood, even in the face of lusty outside influences. Thus, it is not at all likely that a patient will relinquish his individuality to a psychotherapist, even when he has a tugging impulse to do so.

Genuine psychological independence is ordinarily enhanced rather than undermined in successful psychotherapy because the primary purpose of therapy is expansive self-enlightenment; not, as so many people are led to believe, conformity to the wishes and expectations of a therapist. It is true that a client may come to depend quite strongly upon a therapist for his special insights and understanding of human problems. Ultimately, however, the unique explanations and exciting discoveries which typically unfold in therapy serve to strengthen self-awareness and self-confidence. Perhaps, then, not as paradoxically as one might think, as a person depends in a rather narrow sense upon a therapist's skills and knowledge for understanding himself better, he generally gladly sheds a variety of unwholesome dependencies in other spheres of his life.

Incidentally, if a degree of unwholesome dependency creeps into the relationship between client and therapist, this not uncommon development should be perceived and openly broached by the therapist. This bit of therapeutic assistance will probably serve to reverse or correct the detrimental trend. If the therapist, on the other hand, too regularly overlooks or dismisses such an essential matter, there may be cause for reevaluating the overall value and usefulness of the therapy.

9

don't psychotherapists have their own problems?

Isn't it true that many therapists enter the mental health field in order to straighten out their own problems? If so, how can they help others who are troubled?

Certainly psychotherapists, being full-fledged members of the human race, must deal with emotional stress and conflict in their own lives. Unquestionably, one of the reasons why people choose to become psychotherapists is to acquire a better understanding of themselves and to resolve their own personality concerns. It is common knowledge that psychiatrists, for example, have a rate of suicide that exceeds that of the general population. Moreover, experienced therapists generally agree that there are many practicing therapists who suffer from serious defects of character (not including themselves, of course). It is a frightening fact that there are psychotics and sociopaths, fortunately in relatively small numbers, who are delivering mental health services in offices throughout the country. It accounts for the bizarre and tragic stories of the sexual seduction of psychiatric patients, usually attractive young women, by their therapists, that occasionally turn up in the newspapers.

To return to the question, if the unsavory truth is that therapists, like other folk, struggle with their own emotional problems, how can they possibly help others? First, it is important to concede that there is no human being who is devoid of psychological problems. The problem-free person is a fiction or a corpse, whether it is a psychotherapist or a Nobel laureate we are considering for this dubious distinction. Therefore, we need not agonize over whether a particular psychotherapist has emotional problems or not, since we can be certain that, whoever he is, he will have his share of psychological worries. The crucial points then are: (a) whether a psychotherapist's particular emotional problems are so grave that they will interfere with his ability to understand and help others, and (b) whether a psychotherapist has understood and integrated his own emotional conflicts in such a way that he can put them to therapeutic use by being empathic and sensitive to others who are emotionally conflicted.

Mental health training institutes and licensing agencies throughout the country have endeavored to deal with this issue in several ways. Many training institutes and clinical graduate schools require that their students undergo extensive and intensive personal psychotherapy themselves. Also, the institutes and licensing agencies generally require that neophyte therapists receive many hours of clinical supervision in order to qualify for graduation and state licensure. In addition, most mental health agencies institute policies and procedures for evaluating, on an ongoing basis, the quality of the clinical trainee's services. So there are many legal, institutional and administrative safeguards to protect the public by weeding out of the mental health professions incompetent, emotionally disturbed or malevolent individuals. But keep in mind that these safeguards can at times be porous or non-existent in some communities and, consequently, there are some dilettantes and quacks who are legally qualified and working as "professional psychotherapists."

The emotional problems of psychotherapists may be expressed in several different ways. If a therapist's psychological problems are severe, he may emotionally harm and alienate his patients, in which case, his practice will probably fall off so appreciably that he will eventually be forced to leave the mental health profession. This process is usually accelerated by a natural tendency of patients and therapists alike to discuss the relative merits of the therapists who work in their own community. If a therapist's work is abominable, his professional reputation among former and prospective patients will probably be sullied to such an extent that he will lose his primary sources of referrals, i.e., former patients and colleagues. In this way the social and professional grapevines may be the best safeguards of all, since the loss of a therapist's referral sources is a sure-fire step toward losing his practice altogether.

Therapists' emotional problems may also cause a puzzling and frustrating difficulty when the therapists encounter particular kinds of patients. No matter how brilliant, experienced, competent or kind she is, every therapist seems to be especially discomfited or stymied by certain particular characteristics in her patients. For example, some therapists are derailed by patients who are suicidal; some by patients who deliberately lie, others by the voluble or verbose patient, or by patients who are inordinately silent or passive. It can only be hoped that, if the therapist is aware of her limitations and lack of progress with a patient and cannot surmount a therapeutic impasse on her own, she will consult with a professional colleague who can help her resolve her dilemma. If, after consulting a knowledgeable colleague, she and her patient remain on a therapeutic treadmill, it is probably time for her to gracefully refer her patient to another therapist whose work she trusts.

All therapists, like other people, have "bad" days. If a therapist is in the throes of an emotional trial of his own, he may inadvertently inflict some of his distress upon his patients, perhaps by being inattentive, impatient or snappish. The therapist's best antidote for his occasional shabby treatment of patients is to take early cognizance of what he is doing, understand the reason for his uncalled-for behavior and, if necessary, admit to his patients, with a genuine apology, that his work is not up to par that day. Patients are generally amazingly generous and forgiving of a therapist's occasional letdowns, providing they are not fraudulently led to believe that the therapist's crass insensitivity is in some way their own fault.

10

why don't psychotherapists talk about themselves?

There are several reasons which may underlie a therapist's disinclination to share personal information with her patients. First, psychotherapy is based upon the viable principle that, insofar as the psychotherapy relationship is concerned, the patient and *her* life are of utmost importance, not the personal concerns and goings-on of the therapist. The therapist abides by this principle because the patient requires and deserves a relationship in which she can feel that she, not someone else, is of primary concern. Shifting the content of a therapy session away from the patient's life and toward the therapist's personal thoughts and doings not only squanders valuable time, but needlessly diverts the focus and attention of patient and therapist alike from what is exclusively important to them: the patient's overall experiences and concerns.

In no respect should the patient be distracted from her own thoughts, concerns and actions by having to take the therapist's own personal background, perspectives and sensibilities into account. She is free to say what she thinks, without having to feel that she is misappropriating someone else's time or being inconsiderate of the personal needs of her listener. Since the purpose and goal of psychotherapy is to help the patient learn as much about herself as she can, the therapeutic spotlight, even if it is at times uncomfortably brilliant and uncovering, must remain almost entirely upon her.

Further doubts may spring to mind: "How can a patient ever feel close to or trust someone who remains a complete stranger to her? Aren't all cooperative human relationships predicated upon a mutual sharing of personal information and sentiments? If the therapist withholds personal information about herself, doesn't she necessarily antagonize and estrange her patients?"

Most psychotherapy patients initially experience doubts and reservations about the therapist because she is not known to them as a "real" person. To fill the information void they may question the therapist regarding, for example, where she lives, whether she is married, how much she likes her work, in what ways she solves her own psychological problems, etc.

These questions may be catalyzed by a genuine desire on the patient's part to develop a closer relationship with the therapist. But it is helpful to keep in mind that when one person asks another a question of a personal nature, there may be a great many reasons for the inquiry.

Thus, when asked a personal question, the therapist must decide whether it is more helpful to the patient to receive the factual information she is seeking or whether the patient would benefit more from an open discussion of the possible reasons she wants to know about the "real" person behind the therapist's persona.

Let us take the example of a male patient who asks his female therapist, "By the way, are you married?" Is this patient just casually and irrelevantly fishing for information? Not at all likely. Let's consider some of the dynamic possibilities: (a) he may feel the wish to categorize or pigeonhole the therapist according to his image (positive or negative) of single and married women, (b) if he is having difficulties forming interpersonal relationships, he may envy and feel rivalry with the therapist, thus wanting to ascertain if she is more or less adept than he in establishing intimate, permanent relationships, (c) he may wish to know if the therapist is emotionally devoted to another man, and if so, how she could care deeply about him, the patient, and (d) if his fantasies about the therapist have developed along erotic or romantic lines, his question may be based upon the wish that the therapeutic relationship evolve into an amorous enterprise or perhaps even lead to matrimony.

This obviously is not an exhaustive list of the possibilities which the question "Are you married?" may represent; however, it may give the reader some appreciation for the dynamic significance that personal information about a therapist holds for a patient.

Now, to take matters a step further, how should a therapist reply when asked such a question as, "Are you married?" If she says only "yes," or "no," what has she accomplished? Has her answer fostered greater closeness or understanding between her patient and herself? Has she by this means helped the patient to explore and understand why he asked this question in the first place? It is probable that a simple "yes" or "no" reply will not only frustrate the patient's curiosity, but will also arouse in him an even greater yen (possibly accompanied by increased anxiety) for additional personal information about the therapist.

The patient may then be confronted with several concerns: (1) Now that he has extracted this information from the therapist, how much more should he seek to find out about the therapist's personal life? And where and when should this search end? (2) The imparting of personal information by the therapist without her tapping the patient's reasons for seeking this information may cause the patient to feel, not reassured and emboldened, but instead, snubbed by what he has heard. Recall the male patient who wants to know his female therapist's marital status because he is having sexual fantasies about her. Let's suppose he discovers through his inquiries that the therapist is married, but he and the therapist do not discuss his many reasons for coveting this information. Is it not probable, given his fantasies and wishes, that this information will be a decided disappointment to him? He may view the therapist's willingness to share this particular information with him, not as an act of candor and kindness, but as a gesture of crass rejection. And he may be right, even if the therapist had no such intent! So, in this instance, the therapist, by sharing personal information about herself instead of taking the time or effort to explore the basis for the patient's curiosity, has sapped rather than strengthened the patient's self-esteem and trust. We can see by this example how personal information imparted to the patient by the therapist can become more a psychological wedge than a bridge between them.

Many patients are very aware of how this process works, even when they initially enter therapy. It is quite common for psychotherapy patients to observe, "Although I sometimes realize that I would like to know more about you (the therapist), I also like the fact that you are a relative stranger to me. I feel I can tell you anything without worrying about the possibility of offending you. Your anonymity helps me to feel that I don't have to measure myself against you.

Not knowing the 'real' you gives me the freedom to be myself and to feel even more trusting of you."

The above comments include a reference to the patient's favoring a relationship in which she need not compare herself to another person. It is axiomatic in psychotherapy that whatever a patient learns about her therapist will come to occupy an elevated emotional importance in her mind. Now, let us consider what happens if, for example, the therapist shares with the patient how she solves her own problems, how she enjoys herself recreationally, how much money she earns, what her voting patterns are and so on.

It is likely that the patient will have to contend with this information in a variety of ways. Since she is turning to the therapist for vital and expert help, she will quite naturally, yet perhaps unrealistically, consider the therapist to represent a standard of *personal* excellence to which she herself must aspire. In so doing, she also may feel that she is falling far short of the person (or image) she so greatly admires. She may feel this way because she truly has made inadequate headway in life or because she has so idealized the therapist that she must view herself as worthless and meager by comparison with the exaggerated image she has of the therapist.

In any case, if a patient receives personal information about her psychotherapist and the meaning or significance of this information remains entirely overlooked by the two of them, the patient may not only feel diminished and estranged, but she may begin consciously or unconsciously to bypass in therapy certain important subject areas which relate directly to this information. For example, let's assume that the therapist tells the patient that she, the therapist, is a loyal Democrat, works in her spare hours for the defeat of Republican political candidates and believes that those who support the Republican Party are misguided dupes. What effect does such a revelatory statement have upon a patient who is either an enthusiastic Republican or may even just occasionally vote for a Republican candidate?

Chances are, the patient, under these circumstances, will approach the subject of her own political preferences with some trepidation. Since she already knows her therapist's political predilections, she can realistically expect that her own political opinions will be met with tacit or open opposition. She thus must wrestle with the choice either of incurring the imagined or real displeasure of the therapist by openly discussing her political viewpoints or of remaining politically non-committal. She may unfortunately end up discussing politics with everyone except her therapist.

This hypothetical example illustrates some of the reasons why many therapists prefer to present themselves to their patients as a relatively anonymous "clean slate" upon which the patient may sketch any and all of her opinions and feelings without having to take into consideration the therapist's personal attitudes and behavior as orientating guideposts.

Let us return to the matter of whether the patient ever knows the anonymous therapist as a "real" person. Although a therapist may say little about herself to a patient, in a relatively short time some of the therapist's personal qualities will definitely become a perceptible and weighty force in the therapy. The therapist's warmth, humaneness, concern, respect, attentiveness, patience, perseverance, fairness, humor, empathy, intelligence, and integrity are personal qualities which will have an overriding impact upon the patient.

Although the therapist will have in her clinical repertoire a substantial body of theoretical knowledge and an effective set of technical skills, her *personal* attributes will be selectively perceived and weighed by the patient. Most psychotherapy patients are extremely astute in sifting out a therapist's personal qualities from the theoretical and technical aspects of her professional work. In doing so, these patients come to know their therapists in a deeply personal way. Although they may not be privy to information about their therapists' private lives, they will over a period of time certainly be given the opportunity to determine what kind of persons their therapists are.

It is important, however, to recognize that there are a great many times when it may be necessary or beneficial for psychotherapists to share personal information about themselves with their patients. In time-limited psychotherapy, for example, sharing personal tidbits about herself may especially enable a therapist to help a patient overcome a crisis, particularly if the crisis-ridden patient perceives the willingness of her therapist to be personal as a reflection of the therapist's concern for her. Therapists, however, should be very discreet and selective with respect to how they share personal information with their patients as well as highly attentive to the many consequences, both positive and negative, of their having shed some of their anonymity.

One final word: Many therapists err, not necessarily by refusing to share personal information with patients, but by neglecting to reveal to their patients the reasons they have for remaining closed-mouthed about themselves. Most psychotherapy patients are highly receptive to working with a relatively anonymous therapist, provided they are given some valid explanation or rationale for respecting this therapeutic arrangement.

The therapist who merely denies the patient personal information about herself, without explanation or inquiry, will very likely leave her patient feeling that she has been intrusive or offensive in asking personal questions. Left with this feeling, it is not likely that the patient will continue to ask the therapist questions of a personal nature. And this would be highly regrettable, since the personal questions a patient asks her therapist are powerful clues to the central concerns she has about herself. For this reason, a therapist should ordinarily do nothing that would discourage her patient from asking her personal questions, since she would be foolishly barricading an important pathway to the patient's mind. A therapist who is asked personal questions by a patient may wish to respond in the following manner: "If you have any questions about me, professional or personal, I'd very much like to know what they are. Although I will most likely not answer your personal questions by telling you about myself, such questions are extremely important and can assist us in understanding your thoughts and concerns. In other words, many of those things that you will want to know about me will directly reflect what you want or need to know about yourself. That is why I will tend to answer your personal questions with another question or with an interpretation, rather than with personal information about myself. Ordinarily, the process of finding out what prompts your particular questions about me will be far more important and useful to you in the long run than anything I could tell you about my personal life."

11

why don't many therapists offer advice?

Often a person enters therapy with the hope and expectation that his therapist will tell him what to do to solve his problems. I have frequently had the experience of spending an exciting and worthwhile session with a patient, the two of us closely examining and wrestling with the many causes of his inability to carry out decisions, only to have him ask, just before leaving my office, "O.K., now that I know what hangs me up, what do you suggest I do about it?"

There are many reasons why this request for advice should not be granted. Most people from the time they are small children are drilled with much more personal advice than they need or can use. Thus, even though a person may appear to actively seek and want advice from others, he is apt with good reason to deeply resent being told what to do with his life. Despite this resentment, a person, if he is anxious or desperate enough, may search for personal advice from every possible source. Chances are, the great fund of personal advice he culls from others will only aggravate his feelings of confusion and desperation. For this reason, a therapist may ask the patient who seeks his advice if he has already received suggestions from others regarding his personal problems. If he says he has, the therapist might then ask if he has followed any of the advice he has garnered. The patient may reply, somewhat disgustedly, that the advice given him has been too haphazard and superficial to be of any value. Besides, he might add (if he is being entirely candid), he never takes well to being told what to do.

At this point a therapist might ask the patient how he would feel if he told him what to do. Frequently, a patient will answer by conceding, "Well, I'd do what I wanted to do anyway. I'm pretty headstrong." From this pivotal exchange the patient and the therapist have learned that, although he allegedly wants the therapist's advice, he actually prefers, as he should, to unimpededly make his own decisions.

Some patients, however, react quite differently. They promise to follow the therapist's advice ardently and entirely. Such an unconsciously slavish attitude might prompt the therapist to wonder aloud why anyone would do such a risky thing as to obey someone else so completely and heedlessly. The patient may then remind the therapist of the fact that he is a psychological expert and, therefore, it is in his interest to respect and adhere to his advice implicitly. By now it has become clear that the patient and the therapist are uncovering an important facet of the patient's personality. If he is willing to blindly follow the therapist's advice, even allowing for the good possibility that such advice will be discerning and well-intentioned, there can be little doubt that he also tends to be acquiescent with others who occupy positions of authority in his life. By inviting the dominance of others over himself he is taking a serious personal risk since, in the final analysis, he is the only judge of what he must do for himself. Such an important discovery can be one of the primary rewards a patient will derive from his psychotherapy.

A therapist's abstention from extending advice, then, is based upon his conviction that a person usually is helped far more by gaining an understanding of those insecurities and conflicts that drive him to seek advice in the first place than he is by the provision of advice itself. At best, giving personal advice to another person is ordinarily a weak palliative. As a person develops greater understanding and control of those emotional conflicts which cause him to seek direction and dominance from others, he can become more self-directed and, consequently, feel less bound by the opinions and judgments of others.

Although a psychotherapist is, of course, an expert in human psychology, there are some major differences between asking him for personal advice and, let's say, asking your auto mechanic for expert advice about the malfunctioning of your car's motor or, for that matter, asking your family physician for advice about the malfunctioning of your liver. In the case of your car, perhaps a new motor will do the trick. If so, you would want to be informed of that fact and it would probably make good sense to follow the sound advice of a trustworthy mechanic. In the case of your creaky liver, if your trusted family physician recommends antibiotics or surgery to cure you, it is normally wise to give serious consideration to his advice. Of course, when personal or financial risk looms particularly high, it may be prudent to canvass the opinions of other mechanics and doctors before a final decision is reached. Yet such a decision, although it may have strong psychological overtones (the prospect of a liver operation obviously can induce considerable stress, as can the cost of a new motor), largely remains a practical one. Should I have that operation? Do I replace that old motor? These are practical matters which normally can be resolved on a practical basis.

Not so when it comes to psychological or emotional conflicts. Resolving or "repairing" personality or psychical conflicts is not a tangible or practical task for the most part. Emotional or attitudinal conflicts cannot be resolved by simply replacing, adjusting, excising, lubricating, medicating or "doing" something, unless by "doing" something we mean increasing our capacity to understand what we think and feel. Therefore, when a patient seeks a therapist's advice, the therapist may suggest that, at least for the time being, they attempt to determine, as keenly as possible, what the patient thinks and feels about the subject under discussion. Most people, when they come fully to comprehend their emotional conflicts, will be quite prepared to make their own personal decisions and take responsibility for them, however imperfect and painful the results.

A psychotherapist may be reluctant to give advice to a patient, not so much because he suspects that his advice will not be heeded, but rather because he expects that too often his advice will be readily accepted and compliantly followed. By freely and regularly giving personal advice to patients, a therapist would become more puppeteer than therapist. Patients, in their genuine attempts to comply with the therapist's wishes (perhaps out of unconscious fears of offending him with objections), would not seek to fulfill their own goals and expectations. Since one of the goals of therapy is to enhance initiative and independent thinking, advice-giving should ordinarily be a scarce commodity in psychotherapy.

At the risk of appearing to completely contradict myself, I should indicate that there are some situations in therapy that definitely require a therapist to give advice to his patient. For example, if a therapist believes that a patient is seriously undermining, or misusing his therapy, the therapist may need to advise him constructively on how he could better utilize their time together. Also, there are some individuals who during severe emotional crises lack the psychological wherewithal to make a constructive, safe or beneficial decision. In this case, it may be necessary for the therapist to intervene by suggesting alternative courses of action to the patient. When it is imperative to extend such advice, the therapist should let the patient know as best he can that it is only advice he is giving, not commands. The therapist hopes and trusts that the patient will feel free enough to reject his suggestions without having to take the therapist's personal feelings into account.

In sum, a therapist's willingness to extend advice to a patient is usually determined by the following considerations: (a) does the patient demonstrate a valid need for advice, and (b) would the provision of advice be genuinely helpful to the patient? For example, a therapist would probably readily extend advice to a patient who is a newcomer to the area about the best means of transportation to and from his office. On the other hand, it is highly unlikely that a therapist would advise a patient who is a political scientist about how to register to vote.

12

must i relive
my entire past?

Many persons enter psychotherapy with the mistaken belief that they can derive benefits from the experience only if they are prepared to excavate and relive their entire pasts. Sometimes patients believe that the therapist also expects such stupendous recollective feats from them. Because of such beliefs many individuals feel particularly attracted to the idea of undergoing hypnosis, not so much for the purpose of self-discovery and understanding, but rather for immediately disinterring, reliving and reordering the entire past in order to "get on" with the job of living. Herein may lie a magical wish that a full and rapid disclosure of the past will instantly produce revolutionary changes in the personality.

A capacity to appropriately review, revive and relive the past is certainly a most helpful aid in dealing with the present. For this reason, many therapists encourage their patients to reflect upon and emotionally re-experience the events of their childhoods during the therapy sessions. Obviously, some patients are more resistant to this process than others. Some draw a complete blank when initially encouraged to search retrospectively into their lives. Others remember certain past events vividly and yet find whole important segments of their lives irretrievable. Still others can readily reach back, fetch and relate their past experiences with remarkable specificity, continuity and clarity.

While it can be a valuable personal asset to be able to recall and recount one's past in psychotherapy, this capacity, in itself, is not a surefire guarantee that one will grow and mature from the experience. For instance, many patients, despite being real crackerjacks at recalling large portions of their pasts, have a perplexing inability to connect and apply their past experiences to their present conflicts. On the other hand, quite a number of patients, despite severe and immovable repressions of their past experiences, have an excellent capacity to utilize what little they can glean from their pasts.

A patient I had seen for several years was able to provide me with only a bare outline of his childhood years. Invariably, in response to my inquiries about his childhood, he would see it pass before him like a whirling kaleidoscope, with few distinct or apprehensible parts. Because so much of his childhood was a dreary, uneventful and monotonous treadmill, a kind of pallor was cast over his early years, making it difficult for him to regard any one past event as more important or distinguishable than any other. Yet, despite this incapacity, the patient could make excellent use of psychotherapy. His ability to share openly his feelings and form a strong working relationship with me compensated extremely well for his foggy memory.

To restate the matter, a poor memory of one's past does not necessarily cause a patient to flounder and fail in therapy. The corollary of this point is that a titanic memory does not offer an absolute promise of success in psychotherapy. A person's potential to benefit from psychotherapy will be determined by a large number of personality factors—each functioning in combination with the faculty to remember his past—such as an introspective capability, an innate intelligence and the willingness and strength to persevere in the face of painful ambiguity and adversity.

The prospective psychotherapy patient may find some reassurance in the following point. An inability to recollect the important experiences of one's past is often reflective of psychological repression that has taken place unconsciously as a response to the emotional pain and conflict originally wrought by certain early experiences. Many patients discover during the course of psychotherapy, sometimes to their amazement, that their memory for past events improves immensely. This seemingly mysterious change is really no mystery at all. As a patient begins, perhaps only tentatively at first, to look at his past experiences, he gradually faces them more and more fearlessly and realistically. By facing his fears—naturally with the help of his psychotherapist—he loses some of the anxiety he once felt over the experiences and acquires, as a result, a degree of mastery over them, perhaps for the first time.

As a patient becomes increasingly less fearful of his past, he ordinarily also becomes more curious about and interested in his antecedents. He may come to realize that there are genuine answers to some of his questions about himself residing right there in his own past, if only he dare look for them. So, domino-like, the more he remembers and masters, the more he will want and be able to remember about his life. Not surprisingly, many patients note that as this process accelerates, they will remember more about nearly *everything* they encounter daily, including their work assignments, their readings, their social interactions, their dreams, etc. This shift usually can be explained by the fact that as a person becomes less repressed with respect to his own past, he will as a rule become more open, receptive and alive in the other important spheres of his life; that is, he will become a generally less repressed person.

In connection with past recollections, I have, as Alfred Adler recommended many years ago, often asked patients to tell me their very earliest memory. Most people are able to locate and offer a first memory, although they may harbor some doubt as to its accuracy in terms of content and chronology. It is not especially important that the first memory be a perfectly accurate one. What is important is that the patient selects this particular memory usually because it contains certain incipient themes and images that have been very meaningful in shaping his entire life.

For example, a patient's first memory was a brief image of attending his mother's funeral at age two-and-a-half. He recalled standing in mud in a heavy downpour amidst a group of heartsick and silent mourners. Clearly such a telling and awful experience was indelibly stamped upon this patient's memory for good reason. Since the loss of his mother, he had received only inconsistent and grudging care from parent surrogates. His mother's death obviously left him grief-stricken and bereft, and since no one could or would replace her, the patient's life took a chilling direction at this point. As a child the patient fell prone to severe depression that continued into his adulthood. No wonder that his earliest memory was his mother's funeral. It is also understandable that this memory was suffused with themes of grief, loss and abandonment, since these emotions were the primary sources of the patient's chronic depression.

Finally, it is well to keep in mind that, although a person may recall his childhood experiences as nothing more than an opaque blur, an individual's behavior as an adult is in many respects an outgrowth and, therefore, an illustrative reminder of his earlier life experiences. The everyday actions of a person will provide strong clues to the quality and events of his childhood experiences. For example, an individual who has suffered repeated and vicious physical beatings as a child will perhaps not recall those beatings with any clarity. However, when his temper has been riled, he may tend to react by physically striking out against others. This is an illustration of how a person's behavior (his belligerence and combativeness) becomes a tell-tale clue to the earlier events of his life. Thus, even when such a person has no clear-cut recollection of his childhood experiences, his current behavior can provide a solid dynamic key to the quality of those experiences. A psychotherapist keeps this point in mind when he is treating a patient whose memory for past events is unreliable. This may enable him to at least partially open a door to the patient's past and, thereby, help the patient understand the many reasons for his current behavior.

13

is it true that every little thing has deeper meaning?

asically it is true. Many events that are ordinarily overlooked and considered trivial in our everyday lives take on a new, magnified and more profound significance when carefully reviewed in psychotherapy. Some examples will help to illustrate this point.

A young woman who was studying to be a nurse came to her session quite exasperated. When I inquired about her angry mood, she exclaimed that she had gone through a horrible week. She then blurted out, "This week stool was just too much." She gingerly caught her slip of the tongue and quickly acknowledged that for the last several days she had been caring for an incontinent patient whose fecal mess and stench were disgusting her. At length, she proceeded to discuss how caring for this patient had soured her attitude toward her work.

A talented and successful architect was consistently punctual in paying his psychotherapy bills. After several months of therapy he fell behind a bit in his payments. Judging by his sizable income, I surmised that the causes for delaying his payments were not entirely monetary and so I expressed some curiosity about the matter. The patient at first became quite indignant and accused me of suspecting him of trying to bilk me. I assured him that I was quite certain that he would eventually pay me, as he had faithfully done in the past, but I continued to wonder about this unprecedented delay. Didn't it possibly mean anything more than met the eye?

Somewhat sheepishly the patient finally admitted that it did. Apparently the patient's wife, who had never met me, had taken an immediate and strong dislike to me; on principle, I guess. It was she who paid the family bills. For the past several weeks she had had in her possession postage stamps of only one kind. This happened to be the stamp which was inscribed with, of all things, the word LOVE. It was psychologically impossible for her to mail me a payment in an envelope which boasted a stamp with such an affectionate message upon it. Rather than have me draw false conclusions about her feelings toward me, she had withheld payment until she had a chance to get to the post office. I don't recall exactly what other stamp she eventually used to mail her payment, but I do recall that it contained no felicitous messages.

A bright and sensitive young woman who had been repeatedly sexually seduced by her father during her adolescence would begin each session by placing a sofa pillow over her breasts and lap. This behavior went on for many months despite my many interpretations of what it signified. I also noticed that this patient pronounced my name Armada rather than Amada.

After over a year of therapy, I noticed that the patient was putting aside the pillow more frequently. About this time she began to pronounce my name correctly. I was quite sure that these changes were no mere coincidences, so I took the opportunity to ask her about them. She was clear and direct in discussing what these changes meant to her. She stated that she had come to realize that I was not capable of harming her as her father had done. As for her new pronunciation of my name, she revealed that, although she always could read my name correctly, she felt compelled to pronounce it Armada, since she had perceived me to be equally as menacing as a whole fleet of warships. Although she eventually came to feel rather positively about me, I don't know whether she ever realized or cared that my name in Spanish actually refers to a beloved woman.

These examples illustrate how the microscopic and subtle idiosyncrasies of people reveal during the course of therapy important and far-reaching information about how they think and feel. A thirty-five-year-old bank employee who had grown up in a very authoritarian and oppressive home environment one day joked about my name. He mentally divided my name into two sets of acronyms: AMA and DA. Although I had a fair idea of what he had in mind, I asked him to elaborate on this subject with me. "Well," he said, "you are the American Medical Association. Authoritative, knowledgeable and scientific." I was sure he had not completed the list, so I plied him with the possibility that he also saw me as stodgy, conservative, aloof and overly powerful, a common image of the AMA at the time. With some reluctance he assented that he did sometimes feel this way about me.

What about the initials DA? He said, "You are the district attorney. You investigate my mind and detect what is wrong there." Again I felt that he was being somewhat disingenuous. So, taking his awful childhood experiences into account, I tested him by saying with a smile, "And if I find out what's wrong with you, I might prosecute you and maybe even lock you up somewhere. In other words, treat you like your father did." He brightened a bit and then volunteered that he had many times harbored such fears of me.

Sometimes a seemingly trivial manner of speech can reveal decisive information about a person. One day a man who described himself as being in crisis called me for an appointment. I noticed in the course of only a five-minute telephone conversation that he typically began his sentences with such expressions as "quite honestly," "to tell you the truth, " "I hope you don't think I'm putting you on," "the honest truth is," and "if you can believe this about me." This patient continued to express himself in this manner during our initial sessions. In these sessions he mainly referred to those experiences of childhood when he was distrusted and accused by others (mostly his teachers and parents) of lying and dissimulation. He was constantly made to feel ashamed and mortified over committing quite minor infractions of the rules at home and at school. On many occasions he was unjustly accused of wrongdoing and severely punished for the misdeeds of other children. As he grew up, he naturally developed a dread that no one would readily or unconditionally take his word for anything. This fear of course seriously interfered with his ability to get along with others. From his personal history we can see why this man would feel the need to protect himself in relationships by leading off with such expressions as, "I hope you don't think I'm lying to you."

These examples indicate that in psychotherapy there is no such thing as a commonplace event. Simply because we cannot explain or understand a psychological occurrence does not mean that it holds no special significance. Often, a glance, a yawn, a twitch, a smile, a bobbing arm or leg, a "harmless" joke, a fleeting thought, a change of wardrobe or a new hairdo will reveal more about how a person is feeling than the words he uses to describe his feelings. For this reason, psychotherapists are trained to observe and make sense of these seemingly senseless happenings.

A word or two of reassurance is in order. Many persons approach the prospect of psychotherapy with trepidation because they expect that the psychotherapist will place them under his powerful microscope and uncover some monstrous truths about them. They worry that their feelings and thoughts will be totally transparent to the therapist. They fear that if they stumble or are not completely cooperative and straightforward in therapy, the therapist will bushwhack them by seizing upon their difficulty as an opportunity to demean or judge them harshly.

Competent therapists do not treat their patients this way. A therapist's purpose in attending to the small details and vicissitudes of the human personality is not to "catch" someone at thinking "bad" thoughts or doing "bad" deeds. Rather, his purpose is solely to help the patient become more richly aware of what his attitudes and behavior mean so he can change whatever dissatisfies *him*, the patient, about himself. A therapist who pounces upon a patient over, for example, a slip of the tongue or occasional forgetfulness, as if the patient had just confessed to being an important Nazi war criminal, does not understand the marvelous opportunity for psychological discovery such "commonplaces" offer him and his patient and, consequently, does his patient a serious disservice.

Keep in mind, no one, absolutely no one, is transparent. No therapist is omniscient. Therapists only really know what you tell them and no more. A competent therapist can draw certain important inferences from the subtle behavior of a patient, but his opinions remain only inferences until they are verified or refuted by the patient himself.

14

how can a psychotherapist remember everything i tell him?

Obviously, no psychotherapist remembers everything that his patients tell him. Unless he is gifted with a rare aural memory, he will quite naturally forget many of the facts and events of a patient's personal history. Inevitably, some of the information that the therapist forgets will be important to the patient and, therefore, its disappearance from the therapist's memory and his consequent inability to put the forgotten data to positive therapeutic use will occasionally cause the therapy to lag.

Therapists attempt to counteract the problem of their forgetfulness and confusion in several ways. Some tape record or take notes during their sessions and review these tapes and notes regularly and carefully. Others write summaries of the therapy sessions immediately afterward and periodically peruse these summaries for important psychological clues and explanations.

The most vital source of overcoming the problem of forgetfulness and confusion, however, resides in the therapist's capacity to understand his patient and himself. The ability to recall the details of a person's past and to reconstruct these details in such a way as to make psychological sense of them depends largely upon the genuine and deep interest the therapist has in his patient. If a therapist is, as he should be, profoundly interested in knowing his patient as a unique individual, he will find the significant events of his patient's past to be fascinating and memorable. This does not mean, of course, that the therapist will recall computer-like all the minutia which a patient has communicated to him. It does mean, however, that the therapist will remember a great deal about his patient because the patient's life, including its smallest turns, detours and upheavals, is extremely important to the therapist, personally and professionally.

As a therapist increases his knowledge of a patient, that patient's personality and life history take on a unique relevancy to the therapist. The more the therapist learns about his patient, the more distinguishable that patient becomes from any other person the therapist has ever known. In this respect, the therapeutic relationship might be compared to that of an instructor and his many students. At the beginning of a semester an instructor might look out upon a sea of expectant faces and see only a relatively homogeneous group known collectively as: STUDENTS. However, as he reads their papers, listens to their classroom participation and meets with each student in his private office, the instructor, if he is devoted to the profession of education, will increasingly appreciate each student as a special person, with a unique set of hopes and expectations.

So it is with the therapeutic relationship, with one possible major difference. Since a therapist ordinarily works with patients one-at-a-time and can give them his undivided and uninterrupted attention for a great many hours, he will come to know his patients with an intimacy which is unequaled in most other relationships. It is this deep intimacy, primarily, that enables the therapist to esteem his patient's personal uniqueness and that strongly reduces the possibility that the patient's life history will be seriously forgotten or confused with others, despite its inevitable similarities to the backgrounds of his other patients.

There is an additional factor which helps to minimize the risk that a therapist will forget and, therefore, fail to use the important personal information a patient tells him. Since much of the personal information shared with the therapist is vitally important to the patient, he will quite naturally return to some of the significant events of his past many times, often supplementing his recollections with fresh insights and perspectives. By this means a therapist may be afforded many opportunities to hear about a single emotionally notable occurrence from the patient's past, thus providing him with reminders of it as well as of its overriding importance to the patient.

Nevertheless, a therapist should not depend too heavily upon his patient to voluntarily recapitulate his past. Many of the fateful events from his past are no doubt extremely painful to the patient and, once mentioned, he may wish to banish them forever by omitting them from subsequent accounts of his life. The therapist, therefore, must himself assume much of the onus for remembering as best he can the significant information about his patient's past, from the very moment he first hears it.

There are patients who expect a therapist to exhibit an elephantine memory with respect to even the most trivial matters of their lives. A therapist who is expected by a patient to perform prodigious or superhuman feats of recollection would probably find it useful to explore with the patient the reasons for his unrealistic expectations in order to help the patient deal with the certain disillusionment which follows the pursuit of such perfection in others.

Most often, the wish to have one's life history retained by the therapist in its absolute entirety is based upon a two-fold fear. First, it reflects anxiety that the therapist, should he mentally mislay personal facts about the patient, will be severely hampered in his effort to help him. Thus, the patient fears that he will be left stranded with his own emotional problems.

A second fear, one which plagues many patients, is that the therapist will not understand or appreciate them very much. As a result, such patients will watchfully cast about for various signs from the therapist that seem to indicate that he does care about them. One convenient sign to which such importance may be attached, often in quite an exaggerated form, is the therapist's ability to recall the slightest details of his background. Given such fears and expectations, a therapist who does not demonstrate an exquisite memory for facts and details will be seen as uncaring and depreciating. Such a viewpoint, based solely on a therapist's feats of recall, may be quite unwarranted.

On the other hand, it is crucial that a therapist remember much that he hears from and about the patient, since obviously it is precisely this information that he must psychologically decipher and interpret to the patient, if his work is to have any value. Such personal data as, for example, the patient's name, age, marital status, the number, ages and order of his siblings, his occupation, educational background, the quantity and quality of his love relationships and the child-rearing practices of his parents are, just "for starters," fundamental to the process of getting to know the patient. A therapist who cannot keep straight such salient facts about his patient is likely being woefully sidetracked by his own emotional conflicts and will need to analyze himself carefully to get to the root of this problem.

Several times in my practice I have had something like the following experience. After working for several years with a patient, the therapy was discontinued. A year or two later the patient, beset by new emotional pressures, called to make an appointment. He introduced himself by saying, "Hi, this is L. R., do you remember me?" Considering that I had seen the patient for well over one hundred hourly sessions, the patient was someone I, of course, recalled immediately. By broaching his reunion with me in this manner, he was already unambiguously indicating that he was feeling so depreciated and unloved that he could believe it possible that I, even after spending so many hours in intimate conversation with him, could forget him.

A woman to whom I had provided therapy for several months had excessive difficulty starting her sessions. I surmised that this difficulty might have something to do with our initial contact in the waiting room, so I asked whether there was anything about how I greeted her there that bothered her. With some skittishness she said there was. She then remarked reproachfully that I never greeted her by her name. I just said, "Hi." I asked her what feelings she had about my manner of greeting her. She said that although it might sound silly, she thought that I had forgotten her name each time we met. For a moment I was nonplussed, since I naturally had no trouble remembering her name and did not at all suspect that she would think otherwise. This discussion was soon used to very profitable advantage as we further explored the sources of her self-disparaging feelings, most of which could be traced to the humiliating experiences she had undergone with her friends and family.

In each person's life there are certain climactic occurrences that are of such obvious psychological importance that, once mentioned to the therapist, should not be easily forgotten. For example, a patient who reveals that he had spent three years in an orphanage as a child or had lost his mother due to suicide, deserves to have these facts well imprinted in the memory of the therapist. Again, if a therapist tends to blur or confuse such emotionally charged and vital information, he will need to look inward for some of the causes of his difficulty.

15

what is the role of humor in psychotherapy?

The quality and vitality of a sense of humor can determine how well a person will weather emotional storms. A sense of humor can offer perspective by enabling a person in crisis to gain some emotional distance from his own problems. Occasionally, spotting the comical or absurd aspects of a painful emotional experience can bring relief and hope. Sometimes a bit of self-effacing horseplay can pull a person out of the doldrums. For these reasons, a psychotherapist is always interested in the quality and availability of his patient's sense of humor. However, despite the fact that wit can be of undeniable value to someone in distress, the patient who lacks the capacity for humor need not consider himself a poor candidate for psychotherapy. He more than likely will have many other strengths within his personality that will enable him to make effective use of his psychotherapy experience. Overall, it seems more important for the sake of successful therapy that the therapist himself own at least a passable sense of humor.

It is not especially important that a therapist be a good joke- or storyteller, although if telling jokes or anecdotes is in his repertoire of skills, this talent might come in handy. It is more essential, however, that a therapist be ready to recognize and appreciate the humorous and absurd ingredients of a patient's personal experience, when such a perspective is appropriate (that is, when expressing a lighter commentary about a patient's difficulties will be in accord with the patient's openness to viewing his own problems less grimly). A therapist must, therefore, carefully take into account not only his timing, but to what extent a patient, given his current level of stress and self-preoccupation, is reachable through humor. If he is not mindful of these considerations, he can be accused with complete justification of being insensitive or insulting to the patient. Perhaps the following (admittedly implausible) example will illustrate this point.

Several years ago I worked in a psychotherapy clinic which had an elaborate and inefficient system of billing its patients. This outmoded system was finally revamped and computerized. To each patient's name was affixed a seven-digit code number which was registered in the files of the clinic. The method of treatment, which of course was psychotherapy, was also given a seven-digit code number, based upon its listing in a medical formulary. Each psychotherapist would assume responsibility for billing each of his patients by filling out billing forms with these code numbers. The forms were then transmitted to a local bank that, in a completely confidential manner, processed them through computers and then sent the bills directly to the patients.

Around this time a twenty-two-year-old woman, a graduate student of a school of nursing, entered psychotherapy at the clinic. The patient was extremely depressed and inhibited. Her manner was so tentative that she seemed to wince whenever she spoke. Her mood was one of uninterrupted gloom. Toward the end of the patient's second month of therapy, while preparing one of the weekly billing forms, I inadvertently reversed the code numbers that designated the patient's name with those of the treatment services she was receiving at the clinic. In other words, the services described on the bill, covering a one-week period, would be determined by the code number incorrectly attached to the patient's name (as listed in the formulary), rather than by the code number of the actual services she received.

As a result, the patient soon received a bill which read as follows: 1st Week, Psychotherapy, 2nd Week, Psychotherapy, 3rd Week, Psychotherapy. Services for the 4th week read quite differently. The patient was charged for, as inconceivable as it may seem, the following service: SCROTECTOMY (an incision of part of the scrotum). When I saw the copy of the bill that was returned to the clinic describing the delivery of such an unorthodox procedure, I was at first aghast. If my memory served me correctly, I was certain that I had not performed this delicate operation upon my patient. I then began to fear that she would regard this mistake as either a very tasteless joke or as an indication of some blundering stupidity on my part (which it was). Before too long I began to view this farfetched mix-up as a rather hilarious comedy of errors. I hoped that the patient would also see the ridiculous humor of my charging her for an operation upon her phantom scrotum. Perhaps our sharing this absurdity together would lead to greater rapport between us and help to jar loose some of her depression.

No such luck. The next time I saw the patient she made no reference to the strange item on her bill. I began to think that for some reason she hadn't received or seen the bill. Finally, being unable to quell my curiosity any longer, I asked her if she had gotten her bill. Hesitantly, she said she had, without elaborating. "Did you notice the peculiar item on the bill?" I asked, with a chuckle. Flatly, and with some annoyance, she said it had caught her eye. "What's your reaction to it?" "Well," she went on to say blandly, "I just assumed that someone made a mistake." She then abruptly changed the subject and I thought it best not to pursue it any further at that time. Certainly, the absurd humor of this incident had no therapeutic value to this depressed patient.

This example illustrates the point that a therapist, even if he regards a remark or event to be immensely amusing, cannot always consider this a golden opportunity to begin joking with his patient. He must carefully consider several factors, including the patient's own particular brand of humor, the manner and timing he uses to kid around with his patient and, perhaps more importantly, the patient's receptiveness to being treated with humor, to the extent that this can be determined from what he knows about the patient's current emotional state.

Now I would like to give some examples of how humor has played a relevant and positive role in my practice. A young man who had grown up in a home in which sex was a fearful and little discussed subject quite often felt a painful awkwardness whenever he became sexually attracted to a woman. In order to deal with his sexual uneasiness, he was prone to deny that he felt strong sexual urges toward women. During a session that followed a recent romantic disappointment he announced: "I'm finished with women. I wouldn't be turned on by Raquel Welch if she was standing right in front of me, naked." I lightly quipped, "Are you sure of that? Not even Raquel Welch?" He brightened and, with a knowing smile, conceded, "Well, maybe Raquel Welch." This short risible banter allowed us to move

on to uncovering the defensive nature of his announce-
ment and then to exploring some of the reasons for his
bitter stance toward the opposite sex.

A twenty-five-year-old gay man had just finished
discussing some of his mother's personality characteristics. He pointed out that he considered many of
these characteristics to be more masculine than femi-
nine, alluding to his mother's emotional gruffness, her
physical courage, her severe demeanor and to her non-
intuitive or cerebral approach to human problems. I
then remarked that I thought it rather interesting that
these same characteristics seemed to describe the men
to whom he felt most attracted. The patient thought
for a moment and then sang, "I want a man, just like
the man, who married dear old dad." The patient's
delightful wit gave us both a good laugh and helped
to open up an issue which otherwise might have had
limited value.

A fifty-five-year-old woman who was raised by
rather reserved and censorious parents sometimes
felt it necessary to maintain an overly refined manner
while talking with me. During one session she took up
the subject of her son-in-law, who was being derelict
in his responsibilities as a father to the patient's grand-
child. The patient was very critical of her son-in-law's
behavior and after enumerating some of his faults as a
parent, she concluded her remarks with the following
peroration: "He should be a father to his child. After all,
he had a hand in bringing him into the world." After

a short pause, I said, "I, somehow, don't think it was a *hand*." The patient laughed heartily and stated that she herself had thought the exact same thing immediately after she had made her comment. This lighthearted exchange, and many others like it, enabled the patient more freely to express thoughts that she had been taught as a child were forbidden.

An extremely morose and excitable community college student was generally regarded as a belligerent and intimidating individual by his peers. This man came to therapy irregularly, but usually following an incident in which his hostile behavior strongly offended someone at the college, causing him to be warned or disciplined by one of the administrative staff. Because this unfortunate man had little control over his moods and behavior, I thought it necessary to be very sensitive to the terrible distress these campus predicaments caused him. Throughout our interviews he would rant lengthily about perceived violations of his moral rights and, although he seemed to trust me considerably, he gave me little opportunity to share my point of view about his problems. He was largely impervious to my attempts to tap or lighten his angry and depressed mood.

Toward the end of one of our sessions he angrily asserted that no one respected his intelligence or acknowledged his academic accomplishments. He was, after all, a geology major, and a damned good one. Upon hearing this news, I asked him, "Since you're a geology major, what would you say if I told you that's gneiss (a granite rock, and homophone of the word, nice)?" A broad smile broke out upon his face, the first that I had ever seen there, and he said sprightfully, "I'd say, 'gee,' that's a good joke, since it (gneiss) starts with a gee." The two of us erupted with a good belly laugh and in the moments that followed we shared a closeness which had not been there before. His mood, which I could not dent by other means, began to lift after it was reached through humor.

A very shy, withdrawn and relatively friendless man found it intensely difficult to socialize with others, particularly if he did not know them. He explained to me that he found it extremely hard to make small talk and often felt he had little of importance to say. At social gatherings he tended to be an obscure, almost invisible figure.

After temporizing a few days he accepted an invitation to a party. I saw him a few days after the party. He remarked that he had spent a surprisingly enjoyable evening among relative strangers. I asked him what specifically happened at the party that gave him pleasure. He said that, among other things, a joke he had told was well received. I was fascinated by this account, since I had never heard the patient tell a joke in therapy and, although he was quite witty at times, his joke-telling abilities would be interesting to know about. So I asked him to tell me his joke, if he wouldn't mind.

The joke turned out to be a shaggy-dog story; that is, a longish tale with an irrelevant twist at the end.

The story itself I found highly amusing. But, more importantly, I discovered something about my patient that I had not previously known. He told this intricate yarn with such exquisite charm and élan that I only then realized, even though I had sensed it before, how much he had underestimated himself. With such winsome personal qualities there could be little doubt that if he gave himself half a chance, this exceptional person could indeed form intimate friendships.

I think too that it was an important symbolic gesture that this patient was willing to share his joke with me. A person's sense of humor, or wit, is a personal token of what centrally interests, concerns and amuses him. By permitting me to share in the pleasure of his wit, the patient was extending to me a very personal part of himself and, by this means, letting me know that he wanted a closer bond to exist between us.

One final example should suffice. A thirty-five-year-old gay man who worked as a librarian came to me in crisis, immediately following the break-up of a long-standing love relationship. Although he wanted desperately to tell me about his grief, he initially could not overcome the expectation that I would view a gay relationship with contempt. He thought that I would discount the depth of his grief by regarding his mournful reactions to be less painful than those that heterosexuals experience when their love relationships dissolve.

The patient began his first session with an angry challenge. He said, "Look, before I can tell you anything about what I've been through, I've got to know, what do you think of homosexuals?" I must admit that for a moment I had no idea how to answer such an accusatory challenge. I then collected myself and said, "You know, I guess how I feel about homosexuals is a bit like Mark Twain when he was asked how he felt about Jewish people. He said that Jews were human beings like everyone else. And he couldn't imagine anything worse that could be said about a person."

The patient laughed easily and, disarmed of his hostility, he soon proceeded to bring out the recent difficulties he was having with his lover. Although my use of this quotation from Twain was extemporaneous, it has always been a favorite of mine because it says, in effect, that no group of people should be vilified, or for that matter, glorified, for its differences. I had hoped, as it turned out, correctly, that the patient would accurately interpret my use of this quotation. Perhaps what was most telling was my eagerness to respond to the patient's verbal joust, not with anger or with an apologetic discourse on the plights and rights of homosexuals, but with a humorous quotation from a great and compassionate author whose humane values would be well known to this librarian.

As we have seen, humor can be a strong positive force in psychotherapy, providing that the quality of the relationship between the therapist and his patient permits its judicious use.

16

do therapists have favorite patients?

Therapists are sometimes purported to have a predilection for the patient who has been whimsically dubbed "YAVIS," an acronym for the young, attractive, verbal, intelligent and successful individual. These positive personality characteristics are supposed to be the enchanting prerequisites a person must have in order to undergo psychotherapy successfully. This, of course, is nonsense.

There definitely are times when therapists prefer some patients to others. The reasons for this preference may be many and complex. A patient may be a practiced storyteller whose descriptive tales enthrall the therapist. Certain patients may make evident psychological headway due to their psychotherapy experience, thus giving the therapist the personal satisfaction that her efforts are praiseworthy, giving her a sense of gratitude and a special liking for these "good" patients. Other patients may explicitly flatter and commend the therapist for her personal and professional qualities. A particularly conceited therapist would tend to favor such patients. In short, when therapists begin to favor some patients over others, it is usually because the favored patients are meeting the emotional needs of the *therapist* and, by the way, are not necessarily fulfilling their own needs. For this reason, a therapist who favors or disfavors certain patients must scrutinize the basis of her personal biases in order to restore her work to its proper level of professional objectivity.

It is essential for a therapist to maintain largely positive feelings for her patients in order to help them. For most therapists this is a very attainable objective. Although all therapists are assailed by occasional feelings of hostility and displeasure toward their patients, these feelings in themselves are not cause for alarm or resignation. Rather, they can be beacons to light the therapist's way toward learning something important about her patient. If a therapist discovers that she dislikes or is angry with her patient, there is a good chance that the patient is arousing these feelings in her through a particular mode of behavior or expression of feeling. The therapist uses her own emotional reactions as grist to consider the possibility, for example, that the patient is perhaps treating her with disregard, fear, hostility or suspicion. The therapist can then use her own emotional reactions as clues to the inner workings of the patient's mind and, in the process of carrying out this task, help the patient to gain self-insight. In other words, a therapist entirely avoids the retaliatory attitude of reactive anger and vindictiveness. She converts as much as she can the patient's and her own fear and hostility into a restorative search for understanding. By this means she guards against and withstands any temptation to inflict disfavor upon even the most antagonistic and resistive patient.

So, therapists are not devoid of human emotions, negative or positive, but use their training and self-discipline to understand their patients through what their own emotional reactions tell them about their patients.

It is usually the neophyte therapist who inadvertently "has" favorite patients. Favoritism often does a disservice to the patient who is favored, since the therapist's too friendly attitudes can affect her objectivity. Furthermore, the perceptive patient will soon recognize that the unduly favorable treatment she receives in therapy is somehow linked to an implicit requirement that she return the favors by treating the therapist especially well; that is, that she refrain from unfriendly and uncooperative behavior toward the therapist. Obviously this is an obligation which no patient should have to endure.

Certainly, one of the principal causes of a therapist's loss of appropriateness and objectivity is the phenomenon known as countertransference. In this situation, the therapist reacts to the patient as if she were an important figure from the therapist's past. The more intense the therapist's emotional reactions, and the more the patient actually resembles such figures, the greater the possibility of countertransference responses.

For example, a therapist who had an alcoholic parent is more likely than other therapists to react in an irrational manner to an alcoholic patient. Similarly, the therapist who grew up with a severely depressed parent will most likely have inordinately strong emotional reactions to the depressed patient. The problem is obviously more serious if the therapist reacts in this way to all patients, regardless of their particular personalities.

It is usually the inexperienced therapist who has particular difficulty coping with and overcoming countertransference responses. As the therapist gains professional experience, self-awareness and self-discipline, these irrational reactions are not only better controlled, but are effectively used to understand the patient. For example, if the therapist is feeling crestfallen and hopeless in response to a depressed patient, her own reactions can be used to discover why and how the patient herself has been made to feel hopeless and despondent by others. It is this kind of understanding that at once counteracts and corrects the countertransference responses, and enables the therapist to assist the patient in grasping her own emotional conflicts more clearly.

Therapists should have little trouble acquiring and keeping a firm hold on positive feelings for their patients. The regard, respect and fondness that a therapist has for her patients are unconditional. These attitudes are predicated solely upon the fact that the patient is a human being with dignity and untold potentialities. The patient is entitled to the concern and respect that the therapist accords her. The esteem and respect that the patient receives from her therapist does not have to be won or earned; they are basic human entitlements and rights.

Most therapists discover that the more deeply and intimately they learn about and understand their patients, the more they quite naturally care for and respect them. Although a therapist may at times be sidetracked from her respectful and caring attitudes toward her patients, the firm and intimate alliances that eventually take place between them will probably militate against the need of a therapist to favor or disfavor any of her patients. By basing her work upon these rather universal therapeutic principles, the truly competent therapist will be able to work effectively and enthusiastically with a wide cross-section of human beings, including not only the "YAVIS," but the not-so-young, not-so-attractive, not-so-verbal, not-so-intelligent, and not-so-successful person.

It must be conceded that sometimes a patient and a therapist become seriously mismatched. Somehow the chemistry of their personalities is so emotionally straining for patient and therapist alike as to make the therapy unsustainable. Under these circumstances the therapist should certainly consider referring the patient to another therapist, to one with whom she thinks the patient will be reasonably compatible. The therapist should endeavor to point out that it is not the patient's fault that the therapy failed, but that their lack of success together was attributable to a regrettable misalliance between them.

17

should i
tell others?

The person who is considering discussing her psychotherapy experience with others is advised to be discreet. There are several reasons why a cautious tack might be necessary.

Although most of us would prefer to believe that we live in an enlightened era in terms of our understanding and tolerance of mental health problems, such is unfortunately not the case. There are widespread misconceptions, prejudices and downright falsehoods that abound in our society about psychotherapy and about psychotherapy patients. For example, there is the fallacious notion that psychotherapy is a treatment for crazy people. Or, the equally erroneous belief that a person who receives psychotherapy is weak and shamefully inclined to lean upon artificial and despicable "crutches" in order to get along in life.

Another stigma which families sometimes attach to the use of psychotherapy is reflected in the admonition, "Blood is thicker than water. Personal matters should be kept within the family. It is a disgrace to discuss such things with a complete stranger." Thus, according to this dictum, shame and guilt will smite the person who dares to reveal the dark secrets of family life.

Given the high level of bigotry and mythology that surrounds the subject of psychotherapy in our society, it makes sense for a psychotherapy patient to be circumspect in discussing her psychotherapy experience with others. Prospective employers may regard psychotherapy as a boon to an employee's vocational future; or, they may take the jaundiced view that a person who requires psychological assistance will be a disquieting liability to the industry or business.

Friends and acquaintances may feel that psychotherapy is a fascinating and self-rewarding endeavor and, therefore, commend the person who has the good sense to take advantage of it. Or, they may respond with contempt and insensitivity by criticizing or ostracizing the person who takes personal problems to a therapist, rather than seek the advice of friends.

Many psychotherapy patients discover that informing their family and relatives of the fact that they receive psychotherapy can be an excruciatingly sticky and rugged experience. Family members, particularly one's parents, may irrationally assume a *mea culpa* attitude ("Where did we go wrong"), bewailing this turn of events as emblematic of the harmful mistakes they allegedly made in raising their now "damaged" child. They may even perceive their son's or daughter's decision to enter therapy as an accusation against them and, further, their feelings of jealousy and possessiveness may be aroused by having their child turn to someone else for help. Consequently, they might resort to debunking the therapy and the therapist in a pathetic attempt to regain control and influence over their offspring ("Your therapist doesn't care about you the way we do. He just wants your money. What's wrong with taking our advice and help instead?").

These averse reactions of parents to the psychotherapy of their children are, unfortunately, more common than such positive, encouraging responses as, "I think that it (receiving therapy) makes great sense, especially since you're feeling under so much stress. I hope you find it helpful."

Since the reactions of parents, relatives, friends and employers to one's psychotherapy experience are so diverse and unpredictable, it seems advisable to know something about those persons' sensibilities before sharing this intimate information with them. This selective approach will help a psychotherapy patient avoid some disappointments and distress in her relations with others.

Misunderstandings between psychotherapy patients and their friends, relatives and co-workers often stem from and reflect the essential nature of the psychotherapy experience itself. Psychotherapy is, by its very nature, a highly complex human experience, involving a vast number of constantly shifting emotional nuances and subtleties, many of which are nearly impossible to make intelligible to the person who has not undergone psychotherapy herself. How does one find a way to express fully the multitude of indistinct feelings that cause her to consider her therapy worthwhile, to like or dislike her therapist at certain times or to be especially moved and uplifted by a particular session?

The enormity of this task might be compared to the formidable challenge of verbalizing to another person—particularly to one who has not experienced it—why one has been thrilled by a singularly glorious sunset. How does one go about recapturing in words the myriad textures, configurations and the ever-varying splendor of the sunset while at the same time expressing the many exquisite feelings and impressions that were excited by this wonderful phenomenon of nature? Although great naturalists and literary geniuses may be capable of such verbal feats, most of us would find it very difficult to convert our subtlest sensations and feelings about the sunset into words. So it often is with psychotherapy. Since in many respects psychotherapy is one of the most subtle, intricate and poignant of human experiences, most psychotherapy patients will quite naturally find it rather frustrating, if not impossible, to convey this experience adequately to others.

By the same token, those who have not been initiated to psychotherapy will sometimes be hard put to make sense of this "mystifying" human encounter which they have not experienced firsthand. Because they may be puzzled or made anxious by what they hear about psychotherapy, they may tend to give unsolicited advice or try to offer helpful feedback based upon too little knowledge of the person. This can create confusion and strain between them and the psychotherapy patient and even, in some instances, rupture an otherwise good relationship.

There is an additional reason why patients may need to exercise discretion in discussing their psychotherapy with others. As already indicated, psychotherapy commonly induces powerful emotional reactions in the patient. Obviously, many of these reactions persist in the patient well after the therapy session has ended for the day. Sometimes the emotional pain can become quite acute and overwhelming, particularly if the patient has an insufficient understanding of what is causing her suffering. Due to the intensity of feelings, the patient may be unable or unwilling to delay seeking relief from her emotional upheaval. Rather than postpone a resolution of her conflict until she again sees her therapist, she may turn to others for the purpose of venting her feelings in order to receive comfort and encouragement.

At times this means of seeking help can be beneficial. It possibly can take the edge off the overpowering emotions. There is, however, a potential drawback that may result for the following reasons. Many of the most powerful emotions induced in the patient are in direct response to the therapist herself. For example, the patient may be deeply frightened by feeling strongly affectionate or piercingly hostile emotions toward the therapist without having the foggiest idea why she is reacting this way or what she should do about it. If she is feeling this way about the therapist and does not yet feel open enough to share such feelings in therapy, she may take the matter up with other, "safer" persons of her acquaintance, e.g., friends, instructors, co-workers, etc. This psychological detour is technically referred to as "splitting the transference" or "diluting the transference." In other words, the patient, because she is struggling with mercurial emotions about the therapist, attempts to defuse or dampen the feelings by scattering them through her talks and actions with individuals other than the therapist.

The drawback in coping with the problem in this particular way may result from the fact that each time the patient dilutes her feelings about the therapist by discussing them with someone else, she may also commensurately reduce her chances for taking the matter up directly with the therapist. Since it is usually essential to the success of the therapy that the patient explore and understand, as much as she can, the feelings engendered in her by her therapist, anything that deters her from this goal will necessarily impede her psychotherapy. Therefore, if the patient finds—and she probably will—that discussing her psychotherapy with others conveniently enables her indefinitely to avoid taking up sensitive issues with her therapist, it is in her interest to discuss the matter openly with the therapist. The therapist, most likely realizing that a certain amount of elusiveness is common and expected, will, through their open talks, be able to help the patient understand and overcome the anxieties that are causing her to be unnecessarily indirect and diversionary in therapy.

In sum, although it is not recommended that patients always and absolutely avoid discussing their psychotherapy with others, it is highly advisable for them seriously to consider the possible vocational, social and psychological consequences before embarking on such a course of action.

18

are my dreams important?

Sigmund Freud suggested, with good reason, that dreams are the "royal road" to the unconscious. Although the content of dreams is ordinarily jumbled, bizarre and indecipherable, dreams are a potentially rich source of valuable information about a person.

For one thing, dreams are limitless repositories of our deepest emotions. During our waking hours we psychologically censor and dismiss great chunks of what we feel. But the fact that we do not admit our deepest, most intense feelings into consciousness does not mean that the forbidden emotions evaporate or self-destruct. Those feelings that we deny or banish from consciousness go into hiding in our unconscious.

Since dreams are a panoramic window into our unconscious we find in dreams the emotions that we dared not consciously acknowledge while awake. For example, there are many people who aver quite proudly and sincerely they never feel the slightest anger, even when they are badly mistreated. They believe in and aspire to a state of equanimity in which they can disavow all feelings of resentment and hostility. Yet many such people suffer sleeplessness due to the violent and sanguinary nature of their dreams. How is this possible? Well, it is entirely possible that a person who forbids the natural human emotion of anger (or, for that matter, any other emotion) from entering her consciousness will be compelled to deal with it elsewhere. That "elsewhere" is her unconscious, as represented, in this case, by her dreams. The violent nightmares of the insomniac report nocturnally those emotions that she psychologically refuses to heed during the day.

Before discussing the uses and roles of dreams in psychotherapy I would like to emphasize the following points.

1. Everyone dreams with relatively the same frequency. When we are asleep, our mind awakes to another form of existence. Our thoughts, bodily sensations and emotions do not, like the lids of our eyes, shut down for the night. There are many people who sincerely allege that they never dream. They would be more accurate to think that they simply do not remember the many spry dreams that bound through their minds during sleep. For most people, the content of a great many dreams is easily forgotten, sometimes so completely that it gives one the illusion of not having dreamed at all. Consequently, we tend to think that we have dreamed only when we remember a particular dream vividly. Clearly, some people are more adept than others at remembering and learning from their dreams.

2. Although, as I have already suggested, dreams are a rich wellspring of information about a person's deepest emotions, dreams ordinarily do not play a central role in once-a-week psychotherapy. This of course may vary from patient to patient. For example, certain patients feel little affinity for their own dreams and yet fare rather well in psychotherapy by tapping other emotionally important realms of their lives. On the other hand, there are some patients who have a remarkable capacity to revivify and constructively interpret their own dreams, even in only once-a-week therapy. I might add, parenthetically, that, odd as it may sound, some patients have a tendency to introduce their dreams into the psychotherapy, not for the purpose of enriching their self-awareness, but in order to divert attention from other facets of their personal lives.

In psychoanalysis and other forms of psychotherapy that entail multiple sessions each week, dreams generally assume considerable importance and trenchancy, since such therapies have a greater tendency to reach the innermost levels of one's unconscious than those provided on a once-a-week basis. Also, there are certain types of therapists, such as Jungian therapists, who stress the importance of dreams more than others.

3. Dreams have both a manifest and a latent content. The manifest content is exactly what the dreamer sees in her mind when she dreams. For example, dreams frequently bring to life people who are long dead. Or, it is not unusual to find in a dream two or more objects or persons juxtaposed in surrealistic interactions that completely defy reality. Again, this is the manifest content of the dream.

The latent content of the dream is the symbolic, hidden meaning of the dream. For example, a snake that appears in a dream may actually symbolize a penis. And a light bulb or a soft, rolling hill may represent a breast. Someone who dreams of entering a dark, sinister swamp from which there is no return may be dreaming of her impending death. The dread of death, then, is the latent content of the dream. All dreams, no matter how mysterious or esoteric their manifest content seems to be, have a latent content that underlies and activates the dream itself.

4. Although many of the symbols that appear in dreams tend to be universal (that is, they are shared by virtually everyone), the symbols themselves cannot be well understood unless or until the dreamer's particular psychological associations to the symbols are taken into account. For example, a snake may

represent sexual desires in one dreamer and fears
of venomous, deadly attacks in another. In order to
determine the actual meaning of the dream's symbols, therefore, the symbols need to be considered
within the context of the dreamer's unique life experiences. It is toward this end that therapists commonly
encourage their patients to reflect freely upon the
significance of their dream symbols in terms of the
hitherto forgotten thoughts, emotions and personal
experiences they have had.

5. For the most part the purpose of dreams is the
fulfillment or attempted fulfillment of rational and
irrational wishes. The dream-goal of wish fulfillment is
usually observed in children quite easily. The dreams
of young children that depict them as owning an ice
cream parlor or captaining a space craft are rather
uncamouflaged expressions of wishes to gain access
to delicious food and exciting voyages. However, as a
person leaves childhood behind, her dreams generally
become more complex and abstruse.

It is, however, too narrow a perspective to regard
dreams only as handy vehicles through which we
attempt to fulfill our wishes. Dreams express in their
inimitable manner literally everything we think and
feel when we are awake. All the fears, sufferings, attitudes, pleasures, hopes, instinctual urges, doubts, conflicts, insecurities, hostilities and triumphs that we
experience while we are awake resurrect themselves
in our dreams. Essentially, then, dreams are a conden-

sation of our entire emotional life. It is for this reason that we can count on dreams, if we study them seriously, to provide us with a rich understanding of ourselves and others.

By the way, there is no evidence to suggest that dreams are prophecies or premonitions in the literal sense. Although a given dream may contain certain elements of our intentions to carry out a future act, dreams do not forecast the future any more than does the crystal ball in a carnival sideshow.

Let us now deal with some of the uses of dreams in therapy. When a psychotherapist is told by a fastidious, diplomatic and submissive patient that she is "above" feelings of anger, she has reason to be highly skeptical. The therapist knows that no one is "above" feelings of anger. Yet she also knows it would be futile for her to contradict or argue with the patient's irrational contention. By what means then can she convincingly demonstrate to the patient that she, the patient, truly feels and exhibits anger? Well, one possible inroad to the denied feelings of anger is the patient's dreams. Let's suppose the patient states that she does occasionally dream; however, she attaches little importance to the nocturnal wanderings of her mind. Does she sometimes have nightmares or at least entangled dreams that cause her anxiety? Well, perhaps she does, the patient acknowledges.

At this point it may be possible to have the patient elucidate some of her dreams. Our hypothetical patient somewhat embarrassedly reveals that just the other day she had a dream in which she drove over her boss in a Mack truck. She attempts to laugh off this dream by depicting it, in the immortal words of foolish Ebenezer Scrooge (who vainly tried to blind himself to the meaning of his dreams), as "an undigested bit of beef, a blot of mustard, a crumb of cheese, a fragment of an underdone potato."

The therapist now has leverage to inquire into the patient's feelings about her employer. The patient may persist in denying angry feelings, but the therapist, using the graphic symbolic language of the dream, can justifiably suggest that the dream indicates otherwise. If the patient isn't too isolated from her emotions, she may sooner or later realize and appreciate the fact that she is the true author of her dreams; that her dreams originate in her mind for important reasons and that they are reporting to her, admittedly in an obscure and circuitous fashion, feelings which are endeavoring to enter her consciousness. This brief example may give the reader some indication of how and why a therapist utilizes dreams in assisting her patients in understanding themselves.

Another example, this one from my own psychotherapy practice, may suggest how dreams are applied in therapy for the purpose of helping a patient understand and resolve emotional conflicts. A young woman over the course of several years periodically signaled a moderate wish for a more personal, romantic relationship with me. Ordinarily the patient could quickly grasp the causes and implications of her feelings toward me and had little difficulty in viewing them with genuine humor and perspective.

However, during a period when her personal relationships were in acute turmoil, the patient's emotional attachment to me became more pronounced and more sexualized. Not being especially aware of what was happening to her, she experienced considerable anxiety as a result. In the midst of her heightened agitation she described having had the following dream: "I was in a hilly area when I suddenly came upon a man. I knew he wanted to rape me. I started to run, but the rapist chased me. Pretty soon the rapist caught me and began to ravage me. It was then that I awoke in a terrible fright."

The patient puzzled over this dream for a few minutes and then asked me for a possible explanation. In reply, I lightly asked her if she might consider what happens when you combine the two words, "The Rapist." With a bit of blushing the patient tremulously muttered the word, "Therapist."

Soon after this exchange the patient was openly discussing the fact that she had definitely noticed that she had increasingly felt anxious during our sessions and, although unable to attribute her anxiety directly to sexual thoughts about me, she definitely was uncomfortable with me. She then perceived on her own that the instability of her personal relationships was thrusting her into forming a deeper dependency upon me, along with causing her increased anxieties over the sexual longings fostered by her dependency. Understandably, it was soon after this session that the patient's anxieties about me subsided and her nightmares played themselves out. This example illustrates how dreams and dream interpretations can enable a patient to acquire an understanding and resolution of heretofore unconscious emotional conflicts.

19

what is transference?

The subject of psychological transference is enormously complicated and practically inexhaustible. Uncounted articles and entire books, often espousing conflicting viewpoints, have been written exclusively about transference phenomena. The vast amount of intellectual and literary energy devoted to understanding this subject reflects both its complexity and its central importance to the field of psychotherapy. Consequently, the following condensed attempt to shed a bit of light upon the meaning and role of transference in psychotherapy will necessarily be deficient in scope and depth. It is hoped, however, that this discussion will not do too great an injustice to this intriguing subject and that the reader will be sufficiently stimulated by the following remarks to further pursue his interest in the subject of psychological transference.

Most therapists, when they refer to transference, seem to be talking about a patient's unconscious tendency to form a relationship with his therapist that in many respects resembles and reflects the one he once had with the important people of his early childhood: parents, grandparents, siblings, teachers, etc. This means that many of the feelings, attitudes and modes of behavior that the patient displays toward the therapist will mirror those that he, as a child, evidenced in relation to the significant people in his life. In other words, the drives, fears, hopes, beliefs, fantasies, ideas and styles of behavior originally awakened and shaped by childhood experiences become directed at, or transferred to, the therapist; thus, the term, transference. Although a patient may be conscious of some of his transference reactions, the deeper meanings of these reactions are usually not consciously known to the patient.

Why do transference reactions occur in psychotherapy? There are several reasons why a patient reacts to a therapist as if he were an important figure in his earlier life. First, transference reactions exist in *all* relationships. To one degree or another, the quality of a person's social, professional and love relationships will be determined by the nature of the relationships he once experienced as a child, especially with those people who were emotionally important to him. Consequently, it is only logical to expect that the quality of a person's feelings toward his therapist also will be determined, at least in part, by how he has felt about his parents, siblings and the other important figures of his past.

However, transference reactions can become particularly strong in psychotherapy for several reasons. A psychotherapist, by virtue of his professional role as an expert helper, is an authority (or parental) figure on whom the patient emotionally depends. This childlike dependency can arouse in the patient a range of intense emotions toward the therapist that are inappropriate and disproportionate to the actual relationship that exists between them; for example, the patient may groundlessly suspect that the therapist will entrap or manipulate him. These feelings do not befit the therapist because they are based upon and reflect emotional reactions that originated in early childhood, a period of unparalleled dependency and vulnerability. Because these feelings are largely unconscious, they tend to distort the objectivity of the patient's perceptions of the therapist. Thus, feelings of dependency upon the therapist conjure up long-buried emotions from childhood, emotions that do not entirely correspond with the therapist's actual personal and professional qualities.

A primary source of transference reactions is the overall nature of the therapeutic relationship itself. By consistently maintaining a non-judgmental, attentive, empathetic and permissive attitude toward his patient, all within the protective confines of a quiet and confidential physical setting, the therapist creates a therapeutic atmosphere which at once unclogs and protects his patient's feelings. As this process continues and deepens week after week, the patient will very likely experience an intensification of his emotional strivings toward his therapist. Due to their intensity, the patient's emotions, both negative and positive, will strongly color his attitudes toward his therapist. As a result, the patient may endow the therapist with certain characteristics and intentions that he, the therapist, may not at all possess, or possess only to a trifling degree. Because many of these powerful emotions and perceptions have their origins in the patient's childhood, the intentions and characteristics that he attributes to the therapist will be decidedly determined by the experiences he underwent as a child with those persons to whom he was closest emotionally. Thus, a therapist will often find himself credited or discredited by the patient with certain personal motives and qualities which he simply does not or could not possess. When he encounters such inappropriate reactions in his patient the therapist will need to consider the strong possibility that he has come to represent, to some degree, someone from the patient's past. Unraveling the riddle of who this early "someone" is, and exactly what effect he originally had upon the patient, is usually a time-consuming, intricate and extremely worthwhile task in therapy.

The question might be asked: If psychotherapy commonly induces transference reactions, that is, inspires a patient to develop distorted perceptions of his therapist, doesn't this defeat the purpose of therapy? After all, isn't therapy supposed to help people deal with their personal relationships realistically? Perhaps it would be best if the therapist could rid his patient of his transference reactions by completely and actively avoiding or suppressing them during the therapeutic session. Or maybe he could dispel or correct his patient's misperceptions of him by revealing in each session who and what he, the therapist, *really* is, including his own personal experiences, feelings and motives?

There are usually very good reasons why these tacks do not work especially well in dealing with a patient's transference reactions. First, transference reactions are not especially excisable by *any means*. Rather, each person must perpetually contend, throughout his entire life, with the subtle yet powerful ways in which the earliest perceptions of his parents, siblings, etc., sometimes cloud and distort his perceptions of others. Since transference reactions are a ceaseless aspect of a person's personality, they will not be dispelled or obliterated by a therapist who attempts to avoid or suppress their existence. If anything, a therapist who seeks to do so usually exacerbates the patient's struggle to perceive the therapist objectively, since the patient usually needs considerable help, first, in realizing the mere existence of a transference reaction and, then, in grasping why he misperceives or misrepresents the therapist in the first place.

This brings us to our second point. Transference reactions are not easily or completely dispelled because, in addition to being a perpetual, lifelong part of the human personality, they are largely unconscious in nature. Although a patient may be aware of the fact that he is not perceiving his therapist realistically, he most likely will find it extremely hard to grasp the many unconscious reasons for his misperceptions. For a great many patients it is a formidable undertaking to recognize any palpable link between how they perceive their therapist in the present and how they, as children, once perceived their parents, siblings, teachers and other emotionally important persons.

Since transference reactions are deeply rooted in the unconscious and are a permanent fixture of the human personality, does this mean that each person must helplessly fall prey to their harmful influence? Not at all.

When Sigmund Freud first noted his patients' transference reactions to him, he regarded them as a serious, if not insurmountable, impediment to the treatment. It seemed, at first, that a patient who persisted in regarding the psychotherapist as a personification of the emotionally significant persons of his past would be badly hamstrung in viewing and accepting the therapist as a real person in his own right; that is, as someone who could differ, in important respects, from the patient's past relationships. However, as Freud and countless other therapists later came to discover, the problems associated with transference reactions in therapy were far from insoluble. Rather than an impediment, transference reactions were eventually correctly considered to be a marvelous source of valuable information about the patient. If a patient could be helped to recognize the various ways in which he misperceives his therapist (either over negatively or over positively) and could also learn something about how his childhood experiences determined and formed these misperceptions, he could harvest a rich crop of personal knowledge about himself.

For one thing, he would probably discover a great deal about how and why he misperceives *himself,* since much of what he distortedly ascribes to the therapist will inevitably stem from some of the misperceptions he has of himself. For example, if the patient regards himself as weak and stupid, he will perhaps view the therapist as a paragon of strength and wisdom, although his underlying feelings toward the therapist may very well be similar to those that he experiences about himself, that is, contemptuous.

A second and usually invaluable benefit to be gained from exploring transference reactions in therapy pertains to the patient's other personal relationships. The various ways in which a patient will misperceive his therapist ordinarily strongly suggest how he will also misperceive his own social, professional and love relationships. For instance, if the patient distortedly believes that the therapist is attempting, at every turn, to outwit, humiliate and dominate him, it is all too probable that he will anticipate, and perhaps even invite, such mistreatment in his other relationships.

In other words, the quality of a person's transference reactions to his therapist is a wonderful microcosm of how he essentially views and feels about himself and other people. Thus, what he learns about these reactions in therapy can deepen, sometimes quite remarkably, his understanding of himself and others. By correcting and resolving his misperceptions of the therapist, the patient can change how he feels about himself and his relationships. Viewed from this perspective, transference reactions need hardly be considered an impediment in therapy. Rather, they can be both an essential source of psychological information about the patient as well as a vital catalyst of personal change and growth.

Well, if a therapist does not ordinarily avoid or suppress his patient's transference reactions, how does he put them to therapeutic use? In psychoanalytic psychotherapy he selectively *interprets* these reactions. Based upon what he knows about the patient, currently and historically, the therapist attempts to understand the many sources of the transference reactions and assists the patient through his interpretations to recognize the heretofore hidden meanings and implications of those reactions.

Perhaps an example from my practice will help to illustrate the role of transference reactions in psychotherapy. A forty-year-old high school teacher came to psychotherapy suffering from chronic and profound depression. He had sought throughout his adulthood to form close, sexual relationships with women, but was relatively unsuccessful due to a host of intense, irrational fears. He had generalized fears that women, if given a modicum of leeway, would do him untold harm. He dreaded that he would unwittingly become putty in the hands of a woman. Women, according to his perceptions, would, if he allowed them, manipulate, exploit, envelop, emasculate, punish and devour him. Although he could easily form casual, platonic relationships with women, his great fears prevented him from dealing adequately with the prospects of more intimate, sexual involvement with them.

In reviewing this patient's personal history, his conflicts with women became readily apparent. He described his father as brusque, withholding and highly temperamental. More crucially, he revealed that his mother, throughout his childhood, was ordinarily distracted, overworked, unapproachable and unresponsive to him. When she did attend to his needs for love and affection, she undermined his feelings in the following ways:

1. By trivializing them through comments such as, "Don't be upset, you'll get over it. Go out and play."
2. By deflecting them with such responses as, "You think you have problems. Let me tell you about some of the things I've been through."

3. By attaching thoughts of shame, guilt and retribution to these feelings by making such remarks as, "Be a good boy. Don't do anything bad (sexual). Listen to what I tell you. If you trust other people, they will only betray you and get you into trouble. Not only that, you must be worthy of God. He will punish you if you don't do what I tell you."

Since this patient's feelings were rarely acknowledged or validated, he came to regard them as filthy and malignant. Whenever pleasurable, tender feelings arose, he would feel as if he were committing a cardinal sin. He would attempt, as best he could, to psychologically exorcise these feelings and, if necessary, would withdraw hermit-like into the safe cocoon of his home until his emotions subsided.

During the first several months of therapy the patient developed powerful negative reactions to me. He largely perceived me, in many respects, to be the embodiment of his mother. He often felt that I was manipulative, condemnatory, possessive, controlling, self-indulgent and rejecting. If my comments were lighthearted, he thought I was ridiculing and depreciating him. If I suggested an alternative viewpoint to his, he considered me dictatorial. If I expressed a sense of concern or responsibility for him, he took me to be patronizing, overprotective and henpecking. If, on the other hand, I indicated respect for his autonomy and independence, I was seen as callous and rejecting.

Although for the most part I maintained a patient, neutral and supportive attitude toward the patient, his perceptions of me remained inflexibly negative for some time. Occasionally, it became necessary to explain to the patient the rationales and reasons for my actions, since his doubts about me, mainly emanating unconsciously from his memories of a painful childhood, became too intense and overwhelming. There were other times when it was necessary for me to be explicitly reassuring to the patient, informing him that although he was viewing me very negatively, he had every reason to do so, not because I truly matched his grim perceptions, but because he had been so badly shortchanged and mishandled as a child. I also naturally gave him every opportunity to vent his emotions and to think and say the worst about me, without of course encountering admonishment or retaliation.

Although these efforts at helping the patient were moderately successful in assuaging his deepest fears, they seemed to be relatively ineffectual in assisting him to change and mature. When I was finally able to demonstrate to the patient—through interpretations based upon what he told me about his past—the psychological significance of the enduring linkage between his childhood insecurities and his current emotional conflicts, he was able to effectively understand and change

himself. Until this time his emotional life was undermined by a profound inability to disassociate his childhood perceptions from the relationships he formed as
an adult. Naturally, this made it impossible for him to
feel free, confident and optimistic about his worth and
importance to others.

Over a period of many months my explanations
and interpretations of his attitudes and behavior
toward me began to bear considerable fruit. He would
increasingly recognize the various unconscious sources
for his misapprehensions of me. The more he discovered about the inextricable tie between his earliest
perceptions of his family relationships and his current
views of the world, the more he was able to emotionally separate the two. He gradually came to acquire a
more realistic attitude toward his mother's personal
limitations and, by allowing himself to form a strong
positive alliance with me, he became more open and
spontaneous in his other emotional relationships. By
learning gradually and painstakingly about his past,
he could keep it in perspective and deter it from completely ruling his future.

Although this vignette admittedly provides a
greatly abbreviated and oversimplified description of
the role of transference in psychotherapy, it illustrates
the central importance of this phenomenon to the process that takes place between a patient and his psychotherapist. Although transference reactions usually tend
to distort and impede the objectivity and judgment

of patients in psychotherapy, if properly understood
and utilized by the therapist, they are a powerful and
indispensable tool with which patients can be helped
to grasp and remove some of the unconscious shackles
of the past.

Incidentally, strange as it may sound, transference reactions may take place in relation to animals,
plant life, or may even materialize in association with
inanimate objects such as cars and buildings. The
ways in which a person cares for his pets, plants and
automobile usually have some causal connection to
those experiences of childhood when he observed and
digested how his parents and other important people
cared for such things, or, perhaps more significantly,
how well they cared for him.

A patient of mine attributed much of her impressive personal growth to the psychotherapy she
received for several years. At the inception of her
therapy there was a small, immature plant rest-
ing in a pot near her chair. Throughout the subsequent months this plant grew and flourished. One
day, several years later, the plant was transferred
to another area of the room, somewhat out of the
patient's view. After taking her seat, the patient hast-
ily glanced around the room and without seeing the
plant, inquired, "Where's the plant I've always seen
here?" After I pointed to the plant now situated to
her far left, she smiled and remarked with some relief,
"I'm glad to see it. We have done a lot of growing

up together here." This comment, poignantly true, revealed a warm sibling-like attitude toward the plant, while also undisguisedly disclosing that the patient viewed me as a parent who had caringly raised her.

Most of us also develop powerful transference reactions to the home or apartment in which we live as well as toward the facility in which we work. Our attitudes and adaptations toward our home and place of work often reflect and emanate from the emotional atmosphere of the home in which we grew up. It is interesting to note that many patients in psychotherapy will develop powerful transference reactions, not just to the psychotherapist himself, but also to the physical setting or building in which he works. This has sometimes been jokingly referred to as an "Edifice Complex."

20

how do my defense
mechanisms work?

Every second of every day the human personality must struggle with both internal and external stimuli and influences. Internally, our aggressive and sexual impulses are busily seeking outlets and gratifications. Although we may not devote a great deal of conscious thought and attention to our instinctual drives, the fact that we are continually assailed by them is borne out by, for example, an unexpected and seemingly unprovoked loss of temper, an overwhelming hunger pang, a turbulent sexual urge, or an inexplicable violent nightmare. Coping with these instinctual drives is in itself a full-time job, with few fringe benefits such as vacations or leaves-of-absence.

Now let us add to the colossal demands imposed upon us by our instincts an infinite number of external pressures and challenges to our sense of selfhood. Financial insecurities, educational and career considerations, ethnic, racial and sex discrimination, the emotional expectations of family and friends and the many environmental insults with which contemporary society bombards large numbers of persons (e.g., air pollution, congested highways, crowded housing and the specter of international terrorism) may serve to disrupt one's personal equilibrium. Considering the vast number of incessant inner and social forces with which a person must contend, one might sensibly ask, "How on earth do we manage to get through a day without going haywire?"

Well, the fact is that some people do collapse emotionally under the weight of severe psychological stress. However, fortunately, most do not. One important reason why most persons do not lose their psychological equilibrium is their rather automatic and largely unconscious reliance upon defense mechanisms. Defense mechanisms, referred to by one writer as security operations, are a natural and indispensable part of our personality apparatus. By employing defense mechanisms, for the most part without conscious effort or intent, the human personality is able to cope with the emotional shocks and discombobulations it ordinarily receives throughout the course of a day. That's the good news. The bad news is that, from time to time, these defense mechanisms become rusty and may break down, causing a person to feel highly susceptible to the forceful surge of his emotions; perhaps even tyrannized by his powerful feelings. Or, the defense mechanisms may work overtime and become highly rigid, too severely isolating the person from his own emotions and thereby undermining his ability to be emotionally spontaneous, responsive and intimate with others. Perhaps the following discussion of specific defense mechanisms will shed light on their adaptive and maladaptive characteristics.

Rationalization

Rationalization is probably the most perceptible and malleable of the defense mechanisms. But what do we mean when we say someone is rationalizing? Essentially, we are referring to the tendency of a person unconsciously to excuse or justify the consequences of his own actions. What makes this psychological maneuver necessary? The tendency to rationalize one's own behavior or feelings usually stems from the emotional pain brought on by embarrassment, humiliation, deprivation, defeat and disappointment.

A few examples may illuminate this point. Two basketball teams compete for the league championship. Team B loses the crucial game. One of the Team B players remarks after the game that, "We would have won if it weren't for the lousy referee."

This remark was made despite the fact that the officiating was eminently careful and fair. It is designed to provide consolation and recovery from the pain of defeat, if only temporarily.

A young, ambitious man vies for a highly attractive position in his firm. After several months the position is finally bestowed upon his fiercest competitor. Although the competitor, in this case, was clearly selected on the basis of merit, the ambitious young fellow comments, "That horse's ass got the job because of pull. He's been kowtowing to the boss for years." Again, an attempt at repairing and assuaging the hurt of personal disappointment and loss.

One final example of rationalization will suffice. A young boy behaves disruptively at the dinner table. The highlight of this dinner is to be a superb ice cream sundae. His parents threaten the boy with the possibility that he will be sent to bed without having the magnificent dessert. For whatever reason the boy persists in annoying his parents and soon he is banished to his room. Now he must try to fall asleep while remembering what a terrific treat he has sacrificed for the momentary pleasure of ruffling his parents' feathers. How does he manage to sleep in such a state of disappointment?

Aside from the entirely plausible option of raiding the refrigerator later in the evening, it is likely that he will rationalize the sense of profound loss by having some of the following thoughts: "That ice cream wasn't so special. Besides, there are always going to be more ice cream sundaes in the future. When I grow up I'll buy as many ice cream sundaes as I like. I may even own an ice cream factory." Such rationalizations will of course not entirely quell the painful regrets of this child, but they may serve to diminish his sense of loss and thereby enable him to get a good night's rest.

Unfortunately, however, some people meet with too many privations and debasements over their lifetime and, as a result, tend to rationalize their hurts excessively. They may even cease to strive or aspire for self-betterment because, as they put it, "What's the use of trying, I'm not going to attain my goals. My hopes will only lead to disappointment again." Thus, repeated and harsh disappointments and rebuffs can destroy hope and in time a person's ever-ready tendency to rationalize can become an entrenched and self-defeating trait of his personality.

Repression

Repression is the tendency unconsciously to forget or shut out troublesome thoughts and feelings. As we have already discussed, throughout each day, every day of our lives, we are bombarded with an infinite number of inner and environmental forces. In order to forge ahead and meet the customary demands of life, we must selectively distill, censor, ignore and inter much of what we actually experience, mainly unconsciously. If we paid full attention to the myriad pressures and stimuli which continually beset us, we would supersonically run amok.

So it is of psychological necessity that we rather automatically screen and filter what we experience. By this means we can constructively attend to those matters which most require our attention and care; that is, we rather naturally and unconsciously organize our emotional demands and needs. For example, if listening attentively to a long lecture on an empty stomach is more important than immediately satisfying our hunger, we will probably repress our desire for a hamburger at least long and forcefully enough to learn something useful from the lecture. In this manner repression may enable us to concentrate upon and attain a desirable goal.

On the other hand, repression may wreak havoc in a person's life. Forgetting the car keys, a doctor's appointment, important textbooks or a well-known friend's name are all examples of repression which can have tumultuous consequences. These examples usually suggest that one is unconsciously harboring a resistance or aversion to certain obligations and activities. An inability fully to acknowledge such feelings often results in an inner rebellion, sometimes taking the form of passive rather than aggressive defiance, such as when one "forgets" to take out the garbage.

One of the more dramatic instances of repression that I have encountered in my work came to light during a session with a chemist in his late thirties. When this man was a teenager he was badly ridiculed by his peers for a dental anomaly; his front teeth were abnormally long and noticeably protruded from his mouth. He eventually was treated by an orthodontist who filed the teeth down to normal length. However, before he had received corrective dental care, he suffered relentless social abuse for several years. When this man came to see me over twenty years later he had no conscious recollection of either his dental abnormality or of the hellish mistreatment he had received from his peers. Only when I made a direct reference to his adolescent years and the possibility of social difficulty at that time, were these memories awakened and revived. He could then discuss in rather full detail the events themselves and the terrible anguish he experienced as a teenager.

One might ask at this point whether this man's inability to remember his traumatic past was in some way an asset to him. In other words, is it true that "what you don't know won't hurt you?"

Unfortunately, that pithy bit of nonsense is often poor guidance. It was obviously untrue in the case of the man whom we have been discussing. The fact that for many years he did not consciously recall large segments of his past did not mean that his painful experiences during adolescence left no emotional scars. As a matter of fact, his psychological inability to recall and come to terms with his past suffering as an adolescent only served to increase the effects of his current suffering. Thus, this man found it extremely difficult to trust others and was constantly plagued with suspicions that he would be demeaned and ridiculed for his slightest mistakes. The repressed events of the past came back to haunt him without his having the benefit of understanding or appreciating their harmful effects.

Displacement

Displacement is such a commonplace and everyday phenomenon that, like our breathing, it ordinarily escapes notice. Certainly many cartoons have nicely captured the theme of displacement, often with considerable poignancy. For example, we observe the cartoon character who is cowed and downtrodden at work, but who, upon entering his own home, kicks the cat and proceeds to tyrannize his family. Or the reverse may be true: the lordly head of a corporation who is a veritable bulldozer in dealing with his employees, but is a meek and helpless pincushion at home.

The above examples describe the nature of displacement. Essentially then, displacement is the tendency to direct thoughts and feelings that have been aroused or engendered by certain persons, not to those persons themselves, but to others who are more or less incidental to those thoughts and feelings. What makes this peculiar psychological defense happen?

Well, frequently our emotions are aroused by people with whom we feel acutely insecure. If, for example, a ten-year-old boy is constantly harassed and bullied by an authoritarian father, he will unquestionably feel great rage and resentment toward this parent. If he is fortunate, he may be able to express some of his intense anger to his father without landing in the hospital or being grounded to the house for his remaining days. To be realistic, however, very authoritarian parents are quite frightening and, therefore, are also quite inaccessible to such a young child. If these hostile feelings cannot be directly expressed to the offending parent, what happens to them? Do they simply go away?

Not very likely. At home the father-dictator may be boasting that his son holds the utmost respect for him, never disagrees or is uncooperative in his presence. And he is perhaps quite correct, insofar as the child's behavior in the home is concerned. If we pay careful attention to this child outside the home, however, let's say at school, we probably will detect the behavioral expression of intense emotional conflicts. This angry child will perhaps bully and intimidate smaller children. Or he might indiscriminately defy his teachers toward whom he feels unforgiving contempt. Perhaps his emotional conflicts will lead to a completely different course of action. Due to the frightening intensity of his own vengeful feelings he might withdraw from others, become inordinately timid and overconforming. Whether this child becomes overly passive or unmanageably aggressive, either form of behavior outside the home will exemplify a strong degree of displacement.

He may find it difficult to trust those in positions of authority and tend to find an outlet for his hostility by scapegoating those who are smaller and weaker than himself. His unfortunate inability to express or resolve his angry feelings toward his father may become transformed into a general attitude that much of the world is potentially menacing. This attitude is a clear example of negative displacement.

Fortunately, displacement does not always occur as simply or as automatically as the above examples might suggest. The child may be constitutionally strong enough to effectively withstand the effects of his father's onslaughts and, as a result, form positive attitudes toward others. Or the negative feelings his father instills in him may be neutralized or counteracted through the child's other contacts with benign and supportive people.

One of the more glaring examples of displacement which I have observed involved a teenager who pilfered another boy's bike and dumped it into a creek. When this boy was caught and questioned afterward about his destructive behavior he was hard put to explain his motives. His mother, however, mentioned in passing that during the previous week an older boy had taken her son's bike and tossed it into the same creek. A quick check of the chronology of these two events revealed that the second theft occurred, almost to the minute, exactly one week after the first theft. This rather uncanny sequence of events demonstrated how a disgruntled victim can become, through an act of displacement, a retaliatory victimizer.

Incidentally, displacement can and does take positive forms. A child who is treated with respect and kindness by his parents or parental figures will ordinarily give forth and expect those same qualities in his relationships with others.

Projection-Externalization

From time to time our emotional conflicts become so unremitting and self-punishing that, rather than face them head-on, we prefer to cast or "spit" them out. The process of ejecting our problems from ourselves onto other people is known as projection. Some examples of projection are fairly innocuous, even comical. The child with chocolate-smeared lips unhesitatingly declares that it was his sister, Susie, not himself, who broke into the cookie jar. Or, recalling from our discussion of rationalization, the Team B basketball player who blamed the "lousy" referee for his team's defeat. This man was patently projecting his anger and self-blame onto the official. (Incidentally, this example demonstrates that a particular defense mechanism rarely occurs alone or entirely separate from other defense mechanisms. Ordinarily defense mechanisms operate in combination with and overlap each other and can alternate quite rapidly, although usually one particular defense mechanism is predominant at any given time.)

Unfortunately, the tendency to project one's own negative feelings onto others can result in serious personal consequences and even form the basis for the state of mind commonly referred to as paranoia. The intricate chain of emotional events might take the following course. A person develops highly charged affectionate or hostile feelings toward someone else. For whatever reason, these feelings become objectionable or repugnant to the person who owns them. Being unable to acknowledge ownership of unpalatable feelings and the anxieties which accompany them, the person somehow concludes that the feelings are not his own; that is, that they basically belong to the other person. If this tendency remains unchecked, the sense of apprehension may intensify and spread, and in extreme instances a firm conviction may develop that several or many other persons are determined to harm or undermine the individual. So, as the reader will note, from the tiny fertile seeds of self-dislike over one's own abhorrent feelings may grow massive insecurities and conspiratorial thoughts. Such a personal transformation is the result of a projection of self-hatred onto others, thus converting the feelings into an unfounded belief that the hatred really originates in the hearts of one's "enemies."

Incidentally, even when a projection is rampant and results in severe distortions of reality, the person suffering under its effects may be fairly accurate in his perceptions that others are generally antagonistic and forbidding toward him. Since this person so often projects raw and implacable hostility toward others, those with whom he comes into contact may soon come to feel genuine annoyance and disgust with him. Thus, like a self-fulfilling prophesy, a person who tends persistently to blame others for his own hostilities will unwittingly discover that others will surely avoid and dislike him. In this manner he cultivates real adversaries and enemies, thereby apparently justifying his original misperceptions.

Externalization is quite analogous to projection, although it is often viewed as a more conscious process. One generally is externalizing when he attributes his own feelings to forces (not necessarily people) outside of himself. These forces are not imaginary; they do exist in reality. However, when a person attaches excessive importance to their influence over himself, he is employing the defense mechanism of externalization. For example, a man who is debilitated by severe migraine headaches whenever he becomes viscerally angry with his boss might hold the cold (or hot) weather responsible for his ailment. Or a jilted lover might attribute his repeated romantic failures to the wrong cologne or mouthwash, rather than to a lamentable flaw in his personality. We of course cannot deny that chilly (or sweltering) temperatures and bad breath can dampen one's spirits and love life. However, frequently the tendency to blame one's personal plight on such external factors or events is largely based upon an inability to look inward for psychological explanations.

One of the more prevalent and relatively harmless forms of externalization is the currently voguish devotion to horoscopes and horoscopic forces. This convenient means of externalization can be observed in almost any social gathering by casually eavesdropping on the conversation of two relative strangers. A man attempts to meet a woman (or vice versa) by striking up a conversation with small talk. Such an encounter creates a degree of uncertainty and tension. Each fumbles with such questions as: How do I get to know this person? Should I get personal or just discuss sports and the weather? Who is this person anyway, a dud or a gem? What if I get rejected (again)?

Getting genuinely and intimately to know another person is tough work. It ordinarily requires patience, attentiveness, concern, empathy, curiosity, humor and many other personal qualities. Unfortunately, many persons either lack or devalue these qualities in their social relationships. As a result, they seek ready-made, short-cut methods for cementing their social ties. To return to our couple of strangers in the social gathering, a handy vehicle for quickly "discovering" the other person is to ask, "What's your sign?" If the other person reveals, for example, that she is a Scorpio, an illusion is created that something of recognizable substance has been shared by this person. This Scorpio may then be mentally pigeonholed according to those personality characteristics which are horoscopically represented by the sign of Scorpio. If the inquirer happens to reveal that he is, for instance, a Leo, these two strangers can set out to determine on this basis, not only their particular vagaries and quirks, but to what extent they will be amatively compatible. But does this ingenious system work?

When you get right down to it, all that is discovered by exchanging horoscopic signs is information about what time of year a person was born. Then what is the dynamic purpose of such social gymnastics? Largely, it seems, to overcome anxiety and uncertainty. Each person is putting to use an external, peripherally relevant system for understanding himself and others. As a starting point this social gimmick may serve as a useful social lubricant. If it is employed as nothing more than a gimmicky ice-breaker, it can enable strangers to overcome their mutual awkwardness. If such means of externalization are overemployed, however, they will tend to impair self-insight and understanding and thereby produce the undesirable effect of mutual estrangement between people.

Reaction Formation

Reaction formation is one of the more subtle and, therefore, deceptive defense mechanisms. The term reaction formation refers to the tendency of a person to develop a pattern of behaviors and attitudes that sharply contrast with and therefore belie what he truly feels. Let us take the example of a person who wears a fixed and steadfast smile upon his face wherever he goes, regardless of the varying circumstances he encounters. What are we to surmise about this person's actual feelings? Are we to assume that he is always feeling warm and friendly toward others? Probably not. It would be safer to assume that this person is laboring under a fair amount of anxiety as well as anger, but is unable to let his emotional guard down long enough to behave naturally.

As another example, let us consider the person who tromps about with a ferocious expression on his face and generally treats others contemptuously. Are we to assume that this person harbors no tender, empathic feelings? Again, not likely. Obviously such a person is broadcasting considerable hostility. However, a deeper understanding of this individual will probably reveal that some of his hostile facade serves as a smokescreen for a regrettable incapacity to come to terms with the affectionate and intimate feelings he holds. An analogous situation is that of the man who has through rigorous bodybuilding exercises developed a physique that ripples and bulges with muscles. On each of his biceps he has an ostentatious tattoo, one showing a rather menacing battleship and the other a hulking buffalo. This man, to embroider his personal profile further, swaggers when he walks and rides an oversized motorcycle on which he continually seems to defy death. What are we to infer from meeting such a person? Is he really fearless, virile, confident and Herculean in all respects? Hardly.

More than likely such a person is sorely compensating for feelings of inferiority and weakness by acquiring the social emblems and accoutrements that supposedly symbolize personal strength. Rather than acknowledge feelings of powerlessness, he adopts a personality style that *seems* to be emblematic of strength and power.

A thirty-five-year-old man came to therapy with a rather severe depression soon after his marriage ended in divorce. In one of our earlier sessions he proudly and unfeignedly proclaimed that he had felt angry only four times in his entire life. Since it seems humanly impossible not to feel angry at least every fifteen minutes about something or other, I was quite skeptical about the authenticity of his boast. This man suffered enormous physical and emotional torment as a child at the hands of a sadistic stepfather. In church, of all places, his step-father would take his small hands, place them in his own as if in a massive vise, and proceed to squeeze the helpless fingers until the pain became excruciating. As the pain rose unbearably, the boy naturally felt the impulse to cry out. However, his stepfather would then direly warn him that any outcry would result in untold punishment when they returned home.

This young and defenseless boy could do nothing but suppress his pain, his tears, his outcry and, very significantly, his rage. He soon developed a tendency under these harrowing conditions to emit a short, mirthless giggle. The giggle seemed to serve two psychological purposes. First, it somewhat protected him from the vengeful onslaught of his stepfather who brutally insisted upon a stoical response to his savagery. Second, it helped him, to a degree, to delude himself into believing that he was not being tortured and that he was not feeling what he most certainly did feel: murderous rage toward his tormentor.

As he grew older, this man continued to handle grief and anger by stereotypically expressing their opposites, that is, by unnaturally radiating rapture when he was actually experiencing morbid fear and anger. In therapy, whenever he and I discussed his horrendous past and resurrected a vividly painful event, he would expel his short, pathetic giggle as if to say, "Please don't hurt me, I won't complain," or, "See, you can't hurt me. I mock your torment." We see here a form of behavior and set of attitudes (seeming cheerfulness) graphically expressing converse feelings (anguish, anger and dread), thereby exemplifying a reaction formation.

Since people often behave in ways which oppose and belie their inner feelings, one might logically question how we can ever determine whether a person's behavior accurately reflects what he truly feels. In other words, how do we know a reaction formation when we see one? Well, unfortunately, it is sometimes quite difficult to make this determination. One strong clue to the existence of a reaction formation, however, lies in the rigidity and extremism of the person's behavior and attitudes. Perhaps this is what once prompted Gore Vidal to suggest that there might be more scientific value in studying the psyches of fanatical censors of sexually explicit materials than in researching the psychological effects of exposure to sexual stimuli. He no doubt was implying that virulent censors of sexual materials possessed equally virulent prurient interests.

But the essential nature of a reaction formation is usually best discovered *after* this defense mechanism has melted or dissipated. For example, the person who has a gargoyle-like smile chiseled on his face may enter therapy with a vague complaint of feeling "unnatural." After a period of plumbing, acknowledging, expressing and finally accepting some of his "detestable" feelings, this person begins to feel more natural. As personal naturalness flowers, one observes that the beatific smile gradually transforms into a frown or a snarl. As this person gains an even greater sense of spontaneity and sovereignty over his feelings he will probably regain his smile, but with some important differences. The smile will be softer, not as fixed and unflagging, and certainly more expressive of genuine pleasure and self-fulfillment. These impressive psychological strides are dramatic and undeniable evidence of an erstwhile reaction formation that has thawed appreciably.

Regression

Regression is a defense mechanism which is frequently misunderstood and, therefore, much maligned. Regression, as the term is commonly used, refers to the process by which a person reverts to a set of attitudes and behaviors that he formerly held as a child, perhaps even as an infant. As a socially discussed subject, regression sometimes seems to take on some negative or sinister connotations, almost as if all regressive behavior were intrinsically "pathological" and self-destructive.

Actually, our capacity to regress spontaneously may either benefit or undermine us, depending on many factors, such as where, when, how much and for how long we regress. Many forms of regression are quite innocuous and can be actually rather amusing. The staid businessman with the Scrooge-like demeanor permits no enjoyment or informality to enter either his home or place of work. Then one day he decides to attend a corporate convention in a faraway city. Within two days he has gone on a drunken spree, challenged a barroom bouncer to a fight to the death and chased countless skirts with abandon. This weekend respite from his usual Spartan existence can be viewed as a marked form of regression.

Less uproarious forms of regression abound in our everyday lives. Biting pencils, fingernail-gnawing, certain crying jags, hysterical temper tantrums, food, drug and smoking addictions, excessive daydreaming and stress-related and prolonged retreats to bed are all examples of regression.

Usually, when a person experiences a splintering crisis, his capacity to think wholly rationally becomes impaired. He may feel a groundswell of powerful emotions that, because they are unheralded and bewildering, become painfully unmanageable. As anxiety mounts and thoughts become more jumbled and anarchic, the person begins to feel and react as he once did when he was a relatively helpless child. To add to his dilemma he may very well begin unavoidably to recall, consciously or unconsciously, emotions and memories associated with those childhood experiences when he felt particularly impotent and vulnerable. These recollections will of course only increase his feelings of vulnerability and impotence, making the return to psychological equilibrium all the more difficult.

Despite the hazards of psychological regression, the capacity to regress (and regression itself) is often essential to the onerous task of reorganizing and resolving basic personality conflicts. Since most personality conflicts originate in early childhood, it is often necessary to recapture emotionally some of those traumatic events of the past which engendered stress, anxiety, insecurity, guilt, etc. Frequently, the tendency to emotionally block out and forget the past will only increase the likelihood that the traumatic events of one's personal history will thumpingly repeat themselves in adulthood. By emotionally reliving, even partially and quite belatedly, those experiences which produced personal conflict, one may gain some insight into and mastery over the conflict. For this reason, many psychotherapists implicitly encourage their patients to undergo a degree of regression during the psychotherapy sessions. This is usually done with reminders to the patient that he allow himself to unre-strainedly verbalize and emote whatever it is that he thinks and feels, with disregard for the possibility that such behavior might be construed as childish or prepos-terous in most other circumstances.

By acquiring, through regression in therapy, a ser-viceable degree of intellectual insight and understand-ing, a person may then take corrective steps to change his poor self-image and his particular unrewarding style of relating to others. This process of personal-ity growth through temporary regression has been aptly dubbed by psychoanalytic psychotherapists as "regression in the service of the ego." Personal growth through regression does not, however, take place only in psychotherapy. It is quite common for people to gain a distinctive sense of perspective and relief as well as exhilaration after undergoing a regressive experience. Witness the popularity among otherwise "grown-up" adults of gambling, Little League Baseball, neighborhood gossip, and hot tubs. Or, observe the release and solace which a person ordinarily derives from unconstrained crying over the tragic loss of a loved one. To credit regression with the potential for rendering psychological benefit we have even coined some now hackneyed phrases, such as "letting your hair down," "kicking up your heels" and "letting your-self go." These phrases are suggestive of an acknowl-edgment that some degree of psychological regression is essential to maintaining our grip on selfhood.

As suggested earlier, it is also true that some regressive behavior can be self-destructive. Obviously, a grief-stricken person whose regression has taken the course of chronic and intractable alcoholism is likely doing himself irreparable harm. The disgruntled employee whose particular regression is expressed in the form of hysterical and uncontrollable tantrums in the boss's office may soon find himself unhappily among the ranks of the unemployed. The person whose anxiety leads to compulsive overeating (regression) may develop not only health-hazardous obesity, but may also find it necessary to eschew certain pleasurable social and recreational activities. Among the most extreme forms of regression are those psychotic states in which a person loses his grip on reality and is barren of reason and inner emotional resources. Clearly, most acts of suicide are ultimate forms of regression. Here, the destructive effects of regression are unequivocal and everlasting.

So, regression, like the other defense mechanisms, may either propel us toward or deter us from our personal goals. Since regression is largely an unconscious emotional experience, a person will not necessarily exercise ample control over the social circumstances in which he will regress at any given moment. Nor will he necessarily be able to dictate to what degree he will regress or how quickly he will recover from his regression. Again, whether our own mode of regression helps or hinders us will largely depend upon such factors as where, when and how much we regress as well as to what extent we emotionally recover, grow and learn from our regressive experiences.

Idealization

Idealization is the tendency to magnify, glorify, exalt and pedestal the positive personal qualities of others. As a psychological defense idealization takes many forms and serves a variety of purposes. Generally, the person who uses this defense mechanism can be observed assuming a worshipful, deferential and obeisant attitude in his relationships, particularly toward those persons in society who occupy positions of authority.

A person's proclivity to idealize can often be discerned quite readily. For example, usually in my first hour with patients I query them about their parents. Frequently, when I attempt to elicit the patient's opinion or assessment of his parents' personal attributes and liabilities, I receive responses such as the following: "My parents? I don't know why you want to know about them. They're fantastic. No problems. They have a perfect relationship. As a matter of fact they haven't had an argument in over seventeen years."

I will on occasion lightly tease my idolatrous patient by commenting that his parents must be two in a billion and, with obviously feigned amazement, will add that I have never met such perfect individuals in all my years of doing psychotherapy. I might also vocalize my conviction that his parents are unfortunate since their apparent total lack of conflict obviously indicates a grim absence of intimacy in their relationship. If by this time the patient has not reconsidered or relinquished any of his idealized attitudes, I may emphatically suggest that it is no wonder he has felt so miserable. After all, with such saintly, unassailable parents, he must feel like a worthless scoundrel by comparison. With very few exceptions, the idealizing patient will begin to reevaluate and even constructively modify his unrealistic attitudes when they are sympathetically understood and questioned by the therapist.

Idealized perceptions are often found in the attitudes that many persons hold toward the higher-ups of our society, such as employers, supervisors, professors, politicians, doctors, foremen, parents, etc. The higher-up is endowed with magical, omniscient, infallible and indestructible qualities. He is seen capable of performing wonders and is expected to be a bountiful provider and caretaker for those who idealize him. Sometimes the idealized attitude resembles and actually is a form of adolescent hero-worship. The hero is called upon to provide the charisma, leadership, strength and unerring wisdom to rid our lives of wickedness and uplift us in order that we too can perform miracles.

The above description of idealized attitudes offers strong clues regarding the purpose and meanings of this defense mechanism. There appear to be two primary explanations for the occurrence of idealization. First, idealization serves as a buffer or shield against our own rage and contempt. Wherever we find an attitude of unquestioning devotion and awe, we will also meet with underlying feelings of envy, scorn and disdainfulness.

Often a person feels considerable anxiety and guilt over his own contemptuous and murderous feelings, especially when such feelings are aroused by those he ostensibly admires and emulates. Thus, he will unconsciously squelch the loathsome feelings. It is at this point that a significant psychological step is taken. He will elevate those persons who arouse his envy and hostility to the stature of larger-than-life perfectibility and benevolence. Once such "contemptible" persons are placed on a godlike pedestal they obviously become sacrosanct and immune to the wrath of others. The idealizer can then delude himself into believing that he can have no just cause for feeling hostility toward such sublime and indefectible idols. In this manner he denies and controls his rage, thus temporarily fulfilling his original intent, namely, the lessening of his guilt and anxiety. Unfortunately, his sticky problems with others, particularly those in positions of authority, will most likely persist since he has not consciously acknowledged what he genuinely feels.

The second underlying cause of idealization involves the quest to overcome emotional deprivation. When a person is confronted with feelings of emotional emptiness, he often feels an attendant desire to gain restorative nourishment through his personal relationships. If his inner emotional void is profound, he perhaps will feel a gnawing urgency to acquire sustenance from others. But if he is unfortunate enough to discover that his personal relationships provide only paltry satisfaction, he may then be faced with a stressful psychological quandary. Should he resign himself to his feelings of emotional emptiness or should he plug away at trying to extract more gratification from his personal relationships? Actually, since either alternative may be painfully frustrating, he may take quite a different course of action: idealization.

If the emotionally deprived individual cannot induce others to meet his psychological needs, he will at least partially meet his own needs by conjuring up rich fantasies in which he represents others as munificent and nurturing. By glorifying others through fantasy the idealizer can at least briefly imagine and feel that he is being succored and fulfilled. In this way idealization may serve to lessen the painful sensation of inner barrenness and desolation. We should keep in mind, however, that if this means of coping (idealization) with emotional deprivation is used too exclusively, it will probably have little impact upon the idealizer's basic feelings: emotional emptiness and loathing for others.

Altruistic Surrender

Altruistic surrender as a defense mechanism was described by Anna Freud in her book entitled *The*

Ego and the Mechanisms of Defense. She elucidated this defense mechanism by referring to the tragic literary figure, Cyrano de Bergerac. The playwright Edmond Rostand beautifully depicts Cyrano as one who must "altruistically" surrender his love for a woman (Roxanne) because he vainly and wrongly believes that his peculiarly ugly nose must repulse her. This false and unfounded conviction makes it inconceivable to him that his beloved Roxanne (whom he so sadly underestimates) could reciprocate his love. Thus, he decides to champion the love of his principal rival, Christian, who eventually wins, only with Cyrano's help, Roxanne's heart, and marries her. Although he suffers awfully for renouncing his love for Roxanne, he deepens his sorrow by helping his rival masquerade as a brilliant poet and suitor. Why does Cyrano do such a foolish thing? Is he simply a masochist?

Cyrano's "altruistic" surrender to Christian is not, strictly speaking, very altruistic. Basically, he is attempting to steel himself against the terrible prospect of living a barren life of unrequited love. He accomplishes this feat by lavishly assisting a rival who can serve as a surrogate suitor of Roxanne. Although Cyrano seemingly is a paragon of virtue and altruism, he actually is vicariously pleasuring in sensuality and love through the romantic adventures of his unsuspecting stand-in. By seeing matters from this perspective we can better understand the purpose and workings of altruistic surrender: this defense mechanism enables one to gain emotional fulfillment, first, by surrendering to the needs of others and then, by vicariously experiencing the pleasurable achievements of those to whom one surrenders.

We can now see that the term *altruistic surrender* is a bit of a misnomer since the "surrenderer" is neither entirely surrendering his own emotional needs nor is he being taintlessly altruistic in his intentions.

The occurrence of altruistic surrender can be observed in the lives of men and women who, because of serious difficulties in their own love relationships, will zealously strive, like Cyrano, to promote and sustain the love relationships of others. For example, a person who struggles unsuccessfully to develop a love relationship may expend much emotional energy matchmaking for friends. He will attempt to engineer, shepherd and protect the love relationships of friends. In connection with this pursuit he may take a highly voyeuristic interest in the minutest details concerning those relationships, particularly in the romantic or sexual goings-on.

Although this struggling person's plunge into the intimacies of his friends' affairs will probably cause him painful feelings of loss and envy, he may involuntarily continue to surrender himself to others in this way. Why? Because he feels that he can emotionally gain more vicariously than he can ever lose in actuality. By being privy to the innermost thoughts and emotions of his intimates, he can imagine himself in their place and thereby feel to a degree what they feel. Obviously, altruistic surrender yields only limited emotional rewards, but for those who are, for whatever reason, unable to form fulfilling personal relationships, it provides an essential cushioning against feelings of despair and hopelessness. This perhaps explains why so many people are willing to surrender themselves daily to the love making and breaking that takes place in television soap operas.

Intellectualization

When people—especially bright and well-educated people—become anxious, they often resort to explaining and dealing with their feelings through the excessive use of theories, concepts and abstract gobbledygook. Such an attempt to ward off or resolve feelings of anxiety is known as intellectualization. Perhaps this defense mechanism can be explained by the following example.

A fifty-two-year-old woman of obviously high intelligence attempted to impress me in our first hour with her background of culture and erudition. When I inquired about her self-professed tendency to form relationships with sadistic and rejecting men, she immediately launched into a well-formulated and logical explanation concerning her horrible father. At first I was quite impressed with the perspicacity and eloquence with which she described her childhood relationship to her father. I was soon believing that this brilliant person had not only fully grasped the causes of her emotional problems, but was actually on the verge of solving them. I was then rescued by an eye-opening brainstorm. I found myself asking, "Why, if this person so well understands her own psychological problems, does she suffer so greatly from them and come to me for help?" I was amply assisted in understanding this conundrum by my own emotional reactions to the patient. I found myself becoming very bored by her perfunctory recitation of her personal history. I was forced to question my reaction, since I am usually fascinated with how people experience and perceive their childhoods. The answer came quickly. This patient was not emotionally participating in the experiences that she recited to me. In her presentation of the facts she lacked an appropriate amount of pain and emotion. It was almost as if she had rehearsed her spiel and were discussing someone else.

I decided to ask the patient whether she had ever discussed these matters with other therapists and she admitted that she had, many times, with several different therapists. I then inquired as to whether these discussions had ever seemed useful to her, had helped her to change. She acknowledged that they had not been especially useful to her. As a matter of fact, she went on to say, these circumstantial monologues about her past bored her to death. Without revealing that I too was bored by them, I suggested that perhaps there were more pressing matters in her life which concerned her. With a flood of tears she described how her husband, by drinking and womanizing, had ruined their marriage. It is interesting to note that after several months in therapy this patient returned to discussing her past, but with some major differences. Her manner of recounting her childhood experiences became impassioned and, consequently, reviving and reevaluating her past took on a new emotional importance and usefulness to her. Incidentally, I naturally found that I was no longer bored by her recollections.

This example sheds some light on why intellectualization is used as a defense. When emotional conflicts are too painful to face directly, they can be discounted and defanged by explaining them (away) intellectually. If one takes a purely theoretical or clinical approach to his own personality, he can, at least temporarily, wall himself off from the anxiety and pain that is normally experienced when psychological conflicts are considered in more emotional (and human) terms. Although cerebrally excommunicating his own feelings will probably deter a person from greatly enriching his life emotionally, he derives what for him are substantial benefits. First, he inures himself, however tenuously, from emotional pain. Second, he handily deludes himself into believing that he is brighter and wiser than his fellowman. Third, he probably gets away with deceiving quite a few others into believing that he is a superior being who obviously possesses great worldliness. All in all, we see that he uses intellectualization not only to neutralize and control his feelings, but to control others who might perceive and take advantage of his vulnerabilities.

Often, after questioning intellectualizing patients about their personal concerns, I have received replies such as the following: "Well, I regard my problems as largely oedipal. After pondering this matter logically I have come to recognize those phases of my development that are arrested. As Freud suggested over seventy years ago, our childhood experiences are precursors of our adult conflicts. Therefore, I know, given my childhood, that I will encounter certain difficulties with you as my therapist. But I will do my utmost to recognize them as manifestations of projection and negative transference."

This only slight exaggeration of some of the intellectual posturing that occasionally takes place in therapy helps us to distinguish between intellectual and emotional understanding. Obviously, if one understands his own conflicts purely from an intellectual standpoint, these conflicts will be only partially understood and, therefore, will probably persist.

There are several other defense mechanisms which, by arbitrary choice, have not been discussed: splitting, denial, isolation, sublimation, and identification (sometimes with an aggressor). It is hoped that the reader's interest in this subject has been sufficiently piqued that he will read the literature that discusses the defense mechanisms more fully and precisely than can be done in this book.

21

when should i end psychotherapy?

Many patients approach psychotherapy with a fear that it will become an addictive and interminable experience. They hear references to the psychotherapy experiences of other patients that have lasted for many years and appear to become substitutes for life. Thus, they may from the very onset of therapy worry over how they will eventually disentangle themselves from their dependency upon their therapist.

Occasionally, the termination of therapy is imposed prematurely by external factors, such as one party's move to another city or by financial straits. Barring such unforeseen circumstances, a patient who is considering ending his therapy must usually weigh a number of factors.

If the patient's primary concerns have been over certain psychological symptoms such as phobias, inhibitions, depression, etc., he may consider terminating therapy at the point at which he has conquered these symptoms. Patients who undergo short-term therapy commonly terminate their treatment when they have gained an appreciable relief from distressing symptoms.

Those patients who have undergone long-term treatments such as psychoanalysis are more likely to consider terminating their therapy when they have reached a satisfactory understanding of themselves, can face the ordinary demands of life and are capable of developing positive and fulfilling relationships with others on relatively equal terms. Viewed from a slightly different perspective, a patient might legitimately consider termination when his personal strengths have come to perceptibly outweigh his susceptibilities.

There are instances when patients choose to leave therapy, not because they have realized substantial progress, but rather in response to conflicting feelings brought on by the therapy and the therapist. In such a case, a patient may attribute his decision to terminate to the psychological gains and improvements he has supposedly made; however, his actual reasons for decamping are connected to the difficulties he has in dealing with feelings about the therapy and the therapist. Rather than face these feelings by openly discussing them with the therapist, the patient takes flight under the pretext that he is completely well. Since the basic conflicts have been left unresolved, such patients often must return to therapy in order to take up where they prematurely left off.

Others, despite the persistence of acute unresolved psychological conflicts, regrettably refuse to resume therapy, opting instead to struggle in their own individualistic way with chronic emotional pain.

Assuming that a patient's termination of therapy is a natural outgrowth of his progress, the decision to terminate is ultimately the patient's, although such an important decision should ordinarily be based upon and follow a thorough airing of the matter between patient and therapist. Although the plan to terminate therapy may be initiated by either the patient or the therapist, it is in the patient's interest to share with his therapist his many feelings about the experience of ending treatment. The phase of therapy which immediately precedes termination can be a rich and revealing one. Because the impending separation from therapy activates and deepens feelings of loss and bereavement, the patient will need to understand and to come to terms with this experience. Each person has his own idiosyncratic reactions to loss; however, most patients who have undergone a long-term treatment will feel a sense of grief when they terminate which is akin to the mourning that takes place when a loved one dies.

The loss of a love object is the most common cause of depression. Acute grief reactions to the loss of a love object begin in early childhood and continue throughout the course of one's life. Love objects can take many forms, but generally include one's own body, persons with whom one is intimate such as family and friends, pets and even inanimate objects such as a teddy bear or an admired painting. Body parts naturally assume great emotional importance to each individual. Consequently, the impairment or loss of a part of one's body will induce feelings of regret and bereavement. Herein lies the basis for the ritual of the Fairy Tooth Mother who places coins under the pillow of the child who has lost a tooth. This time-honored tradition is based upon a recognition of the need to repair the feelings of loss and lamentation which naturally accompany the loss of a body part.

Of course the death of a loved one such as a friend or member of the family also brings with it feelings of grief. Such a loss may be complicated not only by a sense that one has lost an important source of love, but also by melancholy thoughts that the deceased, through the very act of dying, has actually struck a rejecting personal blow.

Since loss is a common repeated experience which begins in early childhood, personal losses which are incurred later in life have a tendency to revive feelings associated with those earlier losses. For example, a woman whose mother died when she was quite young had denied the impact this death had upon her. Many years later when her dog was killed in an accident, she was flooded with feelings of grief, many of which stemmed from the impact of the initial trauma. In a sense, all adult grief reactions are delayed responses, with the immediate triggering event in adult life exposing feelings that can be traced to early childhood.

When a patient sees a therapist for a prolonged period of time, it is quite common that the patient will develop an attachment to the therapist that is analogous to the emotional ties he once had to the earlier love objects in his life. For this reason, the loss of a therapist due to termination will often symbolize and revive his earlier personal losses, thus deepening his mourning reactions to the termination of therapy.

Under the weight of the grief and anxiety which accompany termination, a patient may temporarily regress, thus showing some of the very same symptoms with which he first entered therapy. The return of these symptoms does not in itself suggest that the patient is in psychological danger or that he has truly returned to "square one" emotionally. These symptoms are merely reflections and reminders of the depth, intensity and importance of a therapeutic relationship that is ending. Since the basic conflicts that originally produced these symptoms have presumably been extensively covered and largely resolved throughout the earlier phases of therapy, usually a relatively brief span of time is required to reconquer these eleventh-hour symptoms.

When a patient experiences perturbation and upheaval in reaction to termination, he can fruitfully explore and test these reactions with his therapist. By gaining an understanding of his feelings about leaving the therapist, he can also learn a great deal about the effect that separations have on him in his personal relationships. For example, if a patient consistently strives stoically to deny feelings of loss over leaving therapy, it is likely that he also denies feelings of regret and dispossession when his personal relationships end. By blocking himself from feelings of grief over personal loss, he loses his appreciation for the significance of his personal relationships. Since loss and bereavement are inherent in human experience, the denial and rejection of such natural emotions can lead to feelings of alienation and emptiness. The ending phase of therapy affords the patient a unique opportunity to express and accept his mourning and, therefore, serves to enrich his understanding of what personal relationships mean to him.

Many patients use the end of therapy as a worthwhile opportunity to review with the therapist their common history. Their best and worst moments together can be reconsidered and appreciated. The patient can express at this time his disappointments as well as his gratifications regarding the therapeutic experience.

For most patients who have undergone long-term treatment, termination of therapy should be discussed and planned for at least several months in advance in order that the patient have sufficient time to integrate the experience emotionally. Some patients may find it especially helpful to end therapy by slowly tapering off their sessions rather than ending treatment cold turkey. This can be done by scheduling sessions on a bi-weekly or monthly basis for a specified time until termination becomes an actuality. In any case, throughout the process of termination it is essential that the patient and the therapist thoroughly discuss the ongoing impact that this significant impending loss is having on the patient.

It is ordinarily sound practice for a therapist to maintain an open-door policy that allows his patient to resume psychotherapy if such a need arises in the future. The patient should feel free to return to therapy without embarrassment or remorse, since one surely cannot predict whether future personal crises will make additional therapeutic assistance necessary.

The patient who terminates therapy will probably be unable to discern and assemble all of the many benefits he has derived from therapy at the point of termination. It is quite common, however, for patients to manifest and perceive the gains acquired in therapy months and even years after the therapeutic experience has ended. For many of these patients the therapist, although he is no longer physically present, remains a telling and vital part of themselves. Since many of the personal fulfillments and rewards one gains from psychotherapy can be quite enduring, in an important psychological sense the therapeutic experience for many people never truly ends.

questions
and answers

Q: I'm considering entering psychotherapy. Tell me, what exactly is psychotherapy? And what is psycho-analysis? Does therapy really work? Also, what qualities should I seek in a prospective therapist?

A: Put in the simplest terms, psychotherapy is a process of interaction between a person expertly trained in human psychology (the therapist) and a person who seeks help with problems of an emotional nature (the client or patient). The process itself can be accurately understood as both an emotionally healing and an intellectually expansive experience for those who are willing and able to put up with some of its occasional ambiguities and frustrations.

By the way, just in case you're interested, psycho-analysis is only one of many psychotherapies that are available to the public. In psychoanalysis, patients are usually seen three to five times a week, lie on a couch while the analyst sits out of sight, are encouraged to say whatever enters their consciousness, and generally pay a rather expensive fee. It's an excellent form of therapy for those who are introspective and can afford the cost.

I regard the following qualities in a therapist to be among the most important.

1. *Respect:* The ability of a therapist to recognize a client's personal worth and right to make his or her own choices.
2. *Empathy:* The capacity to be accurately attuned to another person's feelings.
3. *Genuineness:* The quality of being authentic beyond the role and techniques used in therapy.
4. *Warmth:* The capacity to show concern, appreciation and regard for the client.
5. *Patience:* The ability to listen attentively without judging, oversimplifying or intruding.
6. *Ethical values:* A thorough knowledge of and commitment to the ethical principles of the mental health profession.
7. *Humor:* An ability to observe and communicate the comical and absurd aspects of the human condition.

Although psychotherapy has its detractors who claim that it is no more or less effective than a good friendship, there is substantial evidence to suggest that it works moderately to exceptionally well for large numbers of people. Of course, it is often quite difficult to prove the effectiveness of therapy since some of the major goals sought by psychotherapy clients (for example, increased self-esteem, confidence and hope) are not very measurable. To further complicate matters, we don't know precisely when to measure the progress a client has made as a result of a particular psychotherapy experience. To legitimately determine outcome, should we measure progress during therapy, soon after therapy or many years after therapy has ended?

If you know others who have been in therapy and have benefited from the help they have received, ask them to share with you their impressions of the experience. Then, if you are so inclined, try it out for yourself. In the final analysis, only you can be the judge of whether therapy can work for you.

Q: Following earthquakes, wars and the experience of rape, victims are said to suffer from Post-Traumatic Stress Disorder, a set of psychological and physical symptoms that supposedly follow an exposure to a traumatic event. Could you please explain and describe the disorder?

A: Victims of emotionally traumatic events such as rape, war, torture or earthquakes typically suffer from a wide variety of disruptive symptoms that are collectively known as Post-Traumatic Stress Disorder (PTSD).

Intrusive Thoughts

A common reaction to severe trauma is the tendency to have recurrent, involuntary thoughts that intrude upon one's capacity to concentrate upon and comprehend ordinary, simple tasks. These bothersome thoughts often hark back to the traumatic event itself as if in an attempt to conquer the terrifying effects of the original traumatization.

Unfortunately, for many persons, these intrusive thoughts linger and, like unbidden incubi, enter one's mind during sleep in the form of nightmares as well as during the everyday activities that the victim of trauma pursues. Thus, such thoughts can become a vexing source of chronic sleeplessness and physical fatigue.

Flashbacks

Victims of trauma commonly suffer from unexpected and severe emotional reactions to sudden changes in the physical environment that somehow remind them of the original source of their terror. For example, soldiers who have been in combat amidst heavy gunfire may, upon their return to a relatively safe civilian life, overreact to the loud report of a backfiring automobile. Those persons who have experienced the terrifying effects of an earthquake may react adversely to innocuous sounds and ground-tremors such as might occur when a very heavy truck passes their home.

Generally, when memories and emotions are excessively raw due to a psychologically traumatic experience such as an earthquake, even very slight and harmless changes in the physical environment may be perceived and felt to be dangerous.

A Sense of Personal Fragility and Vulnerability

I suspect that most people at one time or another harbor the emotionally comforting illusion that they are both invulnerable and immortal. Then one day a terrifying event such as an earthquake threatens this false sense of personal imperishability. The traumatic events connected with an earthquake or a war are grim reminders to each of us that one day our lives will inevitably end in death and, although it is not very likely, any one of us could suddenly die as a result of a sudden, unpreventable catastrophe.

Naturally, such a stark realization can be extremely frightening and disillusioning for those persons who have normally hidden from such thoughts.

The Disruption of One's Value System

Over the course of a lifetime most human beings develop a fairly cohesive set of moral and social values. These essential values enable us to determine what is fundamentally important in our lives. For many people, material wealth, status, prestige and power have assumed paramount importance. At times the social values associated with family, friendships, altruism and human services are eclipsed and forgotten. Then, suddenly, a crisis such as an earthquake, a fire or a terrorist attack occurs and the value of human life itself quickly becomes apparent and primary.

As a result, other social values—for example, money, power, status—are, at least temporarily, subjected to greater scrutiny and re-evaluation. In some respects such soul-searching can be healthy and therefore should be welcome as a potentially positive transformative experience.

Survivor's Guilt

Those who survive calamities often come away from such experiences suffused with an immediate sense of relief. Soon afterward, however, one's sense of relief may be supplanted by feelings of guilt and remorse.

Survivors often ask themselves, "How can I be happy when the lives of so many others have suffered devastation?" They then irrationally blame themselves for feeling grateful or privileged at a time which calls for general mourning. They may even think of themselves as bad or evil for failing to mourn sufficiently. In the end, their guilty and remorseful feelings may actually cause them to mourn quite profoundly or to engage in self-destructive behavior.

There are many other disruptive symptoms associated with PTSD, including sadness, irritability, fear of separation from others, a heightened recollection of past traumas and losses, an increase or decrease in appetite, problems at work, social withdrawal, etc. For most people, these symptoms will subside and reach quite manageable proportions within three to six weeks after the initial trauma. If they persist beyond this point, psychological counseling may be in order.

Q: I'm a college student. I think I'm pretty bright and study hard. Yet after studying for many hours, I close my books and can't remember much of what I've read. It makes me feel so stupid. What's going on?

A: This is an extremely common problem among students. In almost all cases, this difficulty has little to do with intelligence. The stressful events in a person's life can cause intense emotional turmoil. This turmoil may unconsciously sidetrack a person from carrying out intellectual and practical tasks. Although you may not realize it, while you are trying to digest your academic assignments, you are probably thinking of something else, some unfinished emotional business, at the same time. Perhaps, for example, it was that nasty fight you had with your mother or father or that criticism you recently received from a friend or from your boss.

In some instances, the inability to concentrate well is due to some form of learning disability. Although this may be quite unlikely in your case, it still may be best to have this possibility evaluated by the appropriate service on your campus.

Q: A dear friend of mine claims to be kicking drugs and has been attending AA (Alcoholic Anonymous) and NA (Narcotics Anonymous) meetings for the past few months. My problem is that she still shows up at my home high on Valium or pot. She thinks I don't notice it, but I really just don't know what to say. I don't want to sound like her mother and ask, "Are you high again?" That will just scare her away. Meanwhile, I am being played for a fool. How do I deal with this?

A: The problem you describe is, admittedly, ticklish, but far from insoluble. If you remain silent about your friend's behavior, it is likely that she will continue to visit you in an impaired state. This means, of course, that her visits will be an emotional ordeal for you. After all, what could be personally rewarding about having conversations with someone whose brain is continually anesthetized and botched by drugs? So, for starters, you might ask yourself whether it is really in your interest to tolerate your friend's destructive behavior for the sake of an already badly damaged friendship.

Also, it might be helpful to realize that, should you eventually decide to tell your friend that you object to her drug abuse, this declaration would not necessarily transform you into her mother. You have a perfect right, as her friend, to insist upon better treatment from her. Keep in mind, whenever your friend visits you while high on drugs, she is not only engaging in self-abusive behavior but, whether you or she is aware of it or not, she is, during these visits, also abusing you with her behavior. You have, I think, an obligation to yourself to put a stop to this form of abuse.

Q: I'm a vegetarian and my girlfriend is not. It hasn't been a problem for the past three years, but now we are thinking of marriage. My dilemma is how to solve the problem of our children's diets with her? She has always said that our vegetarian lifestyle will have to end with our marriage because hamburgers and hot-dogs are easier to prepare and all kids hate veggies.

A: Since your future wife is a diehard carnivore and you eat like a gerbil, you both may have to make a few compromises in determining what to feed your children. If you prefer to deal with this matter largely on a practical level, it might be advisable to consult a dietician or nutritionist in order to formulate a well-balanced diet for the kids. Perhaps a nutritionist could suggest various ways that you and your wife-to-be could combine your favorite foods in their diets without endangering either the health of the children or the marriage itself.

Another approach might be to allow the children, as they gradually develop their own idiosyncratic tastes and preferences for food and the judgment to determine what is good for them, to choose the foods they themselves wish to eat. Assuming that you will raise your children in a reasonably wholesome and loving home environment, I would expect that your kids will eventually exercise sensible control over their own diets, quite irrespective of what either you or your wife want them to ingest.

Try, if possible, to allow the children to develop some autonomy in their eating habits. A sense of autonomy, whether it applies to eating or any other aspect of everyday life, is very essential to the healthy growth and development of children.

Finally, if your kids' eating habits become a serious bone of contention (please excuse the carnivorous metaphor) between you and your wife, it might be advisable to regard this conflict as symbolic of other difficulties and incompatibilities in your future marital relationship. If that is the case, you might find it helpful to get yourselves to a couple's counselor before your relationship begins to vegetate.

Personally, by the way, I think life has no meaning without a good kosher-style corned beef sandwich now and then.

Q: I have a friend who continually lies to me. I don't want to offend or alienate her by accusing her of being a liar but I definitely don't like being lied to. Any suggestions?

A: You might begin by asking yourself if there are any ways in which you may be inadvertently encouraging your friend to lie to you. The impulse to lie is often animated by fear and suspicion. If your friend senses that you will be critical or hostile toward her if she tells you the truth, she may resort to lying as a means of self-protection.

If it is clear to you, however, that your actions or attitudes have little to do with your friend's lying, you will probably be faced with several broad choices. First, you might consider telling your friend that you are aware of the fact that she lies to you and that you regret and resent this behavior. In the interest of your relationship, you could ask her to explain why she has been lying to you. Perhaps such a discussion could help to solidify your relationship—or it might cause it to end, which might not be a tragedy given your friend's tendency to lie to you.

If, following this discussion, your friend continues to lie to you, it may be necessary to face the unpleasant realization that she is simply an intractable liar. If you eventually reach such an unhappy conclusion, you probably should ask yourself if it is truly worthwhile and beneficial for you to continue having such a relationship.

Q: I have developed a pattern of forming relationships with men who don't treat me especially well. Is this a matter of sheer bad luck, coincidence or some form of psychological problem?

A: If you repeatedly enter into and tolerate destructive relationships with men, the likelihood is that you are indeed struggling with a psychological conflict and vulnerability. Oftentimes, such a problem stems from low self-esteem. It is possible that your inability to sufficiently value yourself causes you to seek out and put up with men who are devaluing you.

A problem of this nature often begins in childhood, the formative years, when feelings and attitudes toward one's self first emerge and develop. Commonly, persons who value themselves too little are the children of parents who have inadequately esteemed them. Thus, such children often come to consider their own mistreatment from others as their normal and acceptable lot in life. If this description seems to apply to you, it might be well for you to consider entering psychotherapy as a means of acquiring greater self-esteem.

Q: My friend is always depressed. To me, her life seems great. I tell her to cheer up and be thankful for what she's got. Is this good advice?

A: Frankly, no. Many persons who appear to have no reason to be depressed actually have quite valid reasons for their states of sadness. Although material advantages and comforts can sometimes foster a positive outlook, they are often an inadequate cure for depression. Since depression is frequently brought about by feelings of guilt and low self-esteem, it can, odd as it may sound, actually be aggravated by success and accomplishment.

There are two good reasons you should not tell your friend to cheer up and be thankful for her advantages. First, such false assurances will invalidate her deepest feelings about herself and thereby make her feel even worse. Second, your comments, however well intentioned, will probably and justifiably be perceived as insensitive and therefore might bring about a serious rupture in your relationship with her.

See if you can shift gears a bit by telling your friend that you are sorry she is depressed and that, even though you don't understand the reason for her despair, you are sure there must be valid cause for such feelings. And, as her friend, you would like to help her resolve and overcome her depression. If this tack doesn't work, you might judiciously suggest to your friend that she seek the help of a psychotherapist.

Q: A friend of mine says her sister suffers from Multiple Personality Disorder (MPD). The explanation is that she has two personalities. I've seen both of these "faces" and I think she's faking. What is MPD and how prevalent is it?

A: Multiple Personality Disorder, once thought to be extremely rare, has been diagnosed with increasing frequency beginning in the 1980s. Whether this increase is due to an actual rise in the numbers of individuals who suffer from this disorder or is the result of a greater sophistication and readiness of clinicians and researchers to make such a diagnosis, I don't know. I myself, after many years of doing psychotherapy with a very large number of patients, have only rarely encountered individuals whom I would confidently diagnose as having MPDs.

This diagnosis is usually applied to individuals whose personality structure has broken up and divided into two or more selves. The separate and unintegrated selves are sometimes referred to as "alters" who, in classic cases, may have little or no knowledge of each other. The various alters each seem to comprise a unique facet of one divided self and therefore may sharply contrast from and conflict with one another in moral outlook and social behavior. Researchers are inclined to define the disorder as a survival strategy for the abused child that has become maladaptive in adulthood.

I, of course, do not know if your friend actually suffers from MPD, although I think the likelihood, considering the epidemiological odds, is quite slim. Many individuals display quite different "faces" from day to day, according to variations in mood and circumstance. This does not mean that they actually deserve the diagnosis of MPD. For example, many persons who suffer from sharp cycles of depression will one day appear quite gloomy and the very next rather elated. These faces are not necessarily different alters or personalities, but perhaps merely the outward expressions of contrasting and unintegrated parts of a single self.

By the way, your friend's "faces" are not necessarily faked. I'd check into the matter a little further before making such an unfriendly assumption.

Q: Although my boyfriend and I get along very well, he does something with his friends that I find a turn-off. Whenever he's around his male friends, he engages in name-calling and uses racial slurs. I feel this is immature. Is this something I can expect him to grow out of?

A: You are, of course, quite correct in characterizing your boyfriend's behavior as immature. Also, it is certainly to your credit that you are questioning and objecting to his actions. Evidently, the social values and attitudes of his male friends foster abusive and racist language while they are together. Unfortunately, many men feel virile and macho only when they can scapegoat and jeer at persons of other ethnic and racial groups. This form of childish behavior seems to provide a false sense of adequacy and superiority to those who themselves suffer from feelings of inferiority.

Whether your boyfriend will "grow out" of this form of immaturity depends on several factors. For example, is his racism a deeply ingrained part of his personality or does it represent a transient form of youthful showing off in order to gain acceptance from his peers? If it is the former, the prospects are, unfortunately, somewhat unpromising.

One possible means of helping your boyfriend come to his senses is to tell him how deeply his racial slurs hurt and offend you. You might then suggest to him that if he really cared for and respected you he would give up this self-degrading nonsense. Since, as you say, you generally get along, perhaps such declarations on your part would, over a period of time, sensitize him to the importance of developing a more humane and mature set of attitudes. After all, shouldn't your opinions of his character mean as much or more to him, in the long run, as those of his male friends?

Q: I often procrastinate when it is necessary for me to study for an exam or write a term paper. Am I just lazy, or what?

A: Procrastination is an extremely common problem among students of all ages. Many students mistakenly attribute this problem to laziness, stupidity or simply to a set of bad habits.

On a deeper, more dynamic level, this problem normally originates with an unconscious objection or unwillingness to undertake an unpleasant, externally-imposed demand. The typical student procrastinator, when given an assignment by an instructor, will consciously recognize the importance of fulfilling that assignment in a timely manner. On the unconscious level, however, the procrastinator reacts to an academic assignment by immediately rebelling. If the procrastinator's unconscious feelings could be put into words, they might be expressed as follows: "Sure, I'm supposed to complete this assignment by next week. But nobody is going to tell me when I must complete this work. I'll do it when I feel like it. In the meantime, I've got better things to do with my time."

Because of such unconscious attitudes, the typical procrastinator does not tackle an academic assignment until it becomes absolutely necessary (i.e., the night before an exam or term paper is due). If you are a procrastinator, it might help you to recognize that your procrastination is more a matter of anxious or angry defiance than mere laziness.

Q: My sister says I'm an alcoholic. Although I do drink to excess a few times a year, I don't drink every day. I notice that I tend to get drunk at family parties. How severe is my problem?

A: Because your letter discloses relatively few details about the general effects of your drinking, it is difficult for me to evaluate the severity of your problem. I think it is possible, however, to infer from the drift of your comments that you have reason for serious concern.

First of all, you mention that your sister thinks you are an alcoholic. If you at all trust her powers of observation and judgment, it may be necessary to finally place some confidence in the good possibility that she has a valid reason for using this label to describe your drinking habits. Since individuals with drinking and other addictive problems commonly deny and downplay the seriousness of their own reckless behavior, it is often their closest friends and relatives who have a more objective view of their self-abusiveness.

Your comments that you drink in excess only a few times a year and also tend to get drunk at family parties seem, at best, contradictory and self-serving, unless you rarely attend family parties. I suspect this is a perfect example of an attempt to minimize a problem that has already reached serious proportions and requires help.

According to national statistics approximately 15 percent of college-age males and 5 percent of females suffer from alcoholism, while another 10 percent of males and 6 percent of females in this age group suffer from the effects of alcohol abuse without having moved into dependency. If you at all suspect that you belong to either group, do something about it. Join AA or enter psychotherapy. Now!

Q: If a person displays most of the symptoms of a manic-depressive, is there still a possibility that the person is not mentally ill? What triggers the chemical imbalance that causes manic-depression, and at what age does manic-depression usually appear?

A: It is perfectly possible to display most of the symptoms of manic-depression without actually suffering from this particular form of mental illness. A thorough psychiatric examination and perhaps some blood tests are usually required to establish the diagnosis of a bipolar disorder.

As far as I know, scientific research has not yet identified the specific catalyst of the chemical imbalance that causes manic-depression. At one time, people in the mental health field believed that manic-depression first manifested itself during a person's twenties; now we know that the illness can surface as early as adolescence.

Q: I'm an Asian man and want to know why Asian men are getting such a bad rap for being possessive and domineering toward their women?

A: In a study titled "Selected Acculturation: The Pattern of Chinese-Caucasian Inter-Racial Dating," Chinese-American women were often found to hold a demeaning courtship image of the Chinese-American male. Chinese-American women often reported that getting-to-know-you chatter with Chinese-American men was basically shallow and tended to revolve around common cultural experiences. The females in this study often considered the males to be egocentric (self-preoccupied and self-aggrandizing) and to rarely value women as equal partners in a common dating activity.

The author of the study, Melford S. Weiss, points out that perhaps the Chinese-American male is indeed getting a "bad rap." As he views the matter, Chinese-American females, born and reared in a predominately Caucasian society and subject to the propagandizing influences of American mass media, either consciously or unconsciously accept many American racial stereotypes. Furthermore, according to Weiss, they act upon the assumption that the stereotypes have some validity.

In short, I don't know the answer to your question, and therefore will leave it up to you and your girlfriend(s) to decide who is receiving the greater bum rap. It is ironic, however, that in the phrasing of your question you refer to Asian girlfriends of Asian men as *their* women. Is your use of this possessive pronoun perhaps a Freudian disclosure of the very chauvinistic behavior to which you referred in your question?

Q: Not long ago, my dog died. This has deeply saddened me. My friends say I should have gotten over my grief by now. After all, they say, it was only a pet. They also advise me to replace my beloved pet with another dog. What do you advise?

A: The loss of a beloved pet is an event that will very likely cause profound grief. The attachments and love we feel toward our pets represents some of our best human qualities. The grief you feel over the death of your dog reflects your deep love for it. Therefore, it is unfortunate that your friends trivialize your feelings by saying it was "only a pet."

Give yourself a bit more time to recover from this loss. Then, when the time feels right, go out and get yourself another dog. You are obviously the kind of person who can give a pet a good, loving home.

Q: I broke up with someone and he wants to get back together again. One side of me wants him out of my life and the other side wants to get back together again. How do I make up my mind? How do I know?

A: If you're quite sure that you broke up with your boyfriend for valid reasons—was he perhaps too uncaring, exploitative, unfaithful or simply a colossal bore?—it probably behooves you to listen to the side of yourself that wants him out of your life. The other, more dependent side of yourself is probably feeling rather lonely or guilty and adrift over the ending of your relationship with him. Ordinarily, it is unwise to rush back into an unhealthy relationship simply to overcome feelings of bereavement. Give yourself time to heal and recover from the loss and eventually you will probably find another swain more to your liking.

Q: What's the best way to introduce your latest boyfriend to disapproving parents?

A: Parents may disapprove of their child's choice of a partner for a wide variety of reasons, not all of which are necessarily logical or wholesome. Some parents, unfortunately, tend to oppose anyone their child chooses to date, apparently on principle. Others may be finicky about the physical appearance, ethnicity or income prospects of their child's partner. Of course, parents may also have good, rational reasons for expressing disapproval, such as when their child's partner demonstrates obviously obnoxious or dangerously unsuitable qualities.

If you can, try discussing your concerns with your parents before introducing your boyfriend to them. Keep in mind that, no matter what you tell them, they may still disapprove of him. You might, then, be faced with the tough choice of incurring their disapproval or giving up your relationship. Remember, part of the process of growing up and reaching maturity is being able to effectively deal with the negative opinions of others, including your parents.

Q: My friend is dating a man who is HIV positive. When I try to talk to her about it, she gets defensive. She assures me she's practicing safe sex, but I'm still concerned about her physical and mental health. What do I tell her?

A: AIDS, as you probably know, is transmitted by a virus either through unprotected sex or the sharing of hypodermic needles. If your friend means what she says—that she fully protects herself sexually and does not share needles with her partner—she is probably not in imminent danger.

If you sense that her defensiveness suggests your friend is not practicing safe sex, speak candidly to her about your concerns for her welfare. You might also mention that she can receive helpful advice by calling, anonymously, one of the AIDS hotlines in her community.

Q: I have always been very shy. What can I do to overcome my shyness?

A: Most people experience shyness to some extent. Some individuals are shy in one-to-one relationships, perhaps especially in their dealings with persons who are in positions of authority. It is also quite common for people to feel very shy when they must make a public speech or presentation. Many persons feel acutely shy when they have performed an outstanding accomplishment or received a compliment.

It is important to realize that people are not born shy. They usually acquire this tendency during their formative childhood years. Although overcoming your shyness may, at times, be very difficult or even painful, it is important to keep your hopes alive by realizing that much shyness can be overcome. Try asserting yourself a little at a time and appreciate even small increments of progress in this area.

Q: What's the best way to put out a fire in your heart for your college math teacher?

A: Many students feel strong attachments and infatuations toward their instructors. Sometimes these feelings are based upon the actual positive qualities of the instructors, such as their intelligence and charisma.

Oftentimes, however, many students "fall for" or idealize instructors out of a need for a close relationship with a parental figure. If you're afire over a particular instructor, ask yourself what there is about the instructor that infatuates you. Then consider why those particular qualities arouse your interest. By the way, the personal qualities you find most attractive in the instructor may be the very same qualities you feel are lacking in yourself. In other words, your attraction may be based on a wish to overcome a personal shortcoming by drawing strength and esteem from a parental figure such as the instructor. In any case, do the best you can by exercising self-control and discretion.

Q: I am a part-time college student. My girlfriend has recently left her three-month-old son with me to take care of. She has gone away to live with her parents. My friends and family say that a child needs its mother to fulfill its emotional needs. I am not sure if I have the maternal instincts necessary to raise my son properly. What do I do?

A: I'm not entirely sure there is such a thing as a purely "maternal" instinct. Normally, a child's emotional needs are satisfactorily fulfilled when the parent(s) provide fairly consistent care and nurturance. Be assured many men have an excellent capacity to foster the well-being of children.

If you truly feel that you are a caring and nurturing parent, don't allow others to convince you otherwise. If, however, you have serious doubts about your parental capabilities, it is probably in your interest to join a support group or seek personal counseling before making a fateful decision regarding your son's future.

Q: I'm Catholic and my girlfriend is Jewish-Orthodox. How do we deal with the matter of our two different religions, and what about the kids?

A: Despite your religious differences, there are probably an infinite number of ways in which you and your girlfriend share common and compatible moral values. The primary challenge that awaits both of you is whether you will be able to respect each other's religious beliefs without undue conflict or acrimony.

Couples with strongly contrasting religious backgrounds generally raise their children in one of the following ways: (a) the children are given no religious training or education and are expected to make up their own minds about religion when they reach maturity;

(b) the children are inculcated with the teachings and tenets of both faiths and are then expected to capably reconcile the differences, commonalities and contradictions between the two; (c) the religion of one parent is given predominance over the other in the home. I know of no study that demonstrates the superiority of any given system of handling parental religious differences over another.

Q: What should I do or say as a parent when my little boy comes home from school after getting in his first fight and asks what he should have done?

A: You might begin by simply consoling your son. Being in a fight can be a terrifying and humiliating experience, especially if a child has been on the receiving end of a bad beating. Empathize with your son's feelings of victimization without prodding him into a belligerent and vengeful attitude toward his adversary. Over the course of time, your son will probably learn to defend himself quite well without your advice or direct intervention. Of course, if the fighting continues and becomes severe, you may need to directly intervene by, for example, discussing the matter with the school authorities or the other boy's parents.

Q: When I try to talk to my mother at an adult level, she reduces me to the level of a twelve-year-old. How can I get her to accept me as a mature adult?

A: Many parents tend to infantilize (baby) their adult children. They often do this in order to inflate their own importance. Assuming that you are not now a twelve-year-old, I'd guess that you find this treatment very degrading.

It might be necessary to firmly tell your mother that you resent her demeaning manner. If, despite your efforts, she persists in treating you in a humiliating manner, you may need to plainly insist upon your right to more respectful treatment. Of course, your mother may have a deep and unshakable stake in forever viewing you as a helpless infant. If so, it's probably best for you to devote most of your energies to accepting yourself as a mature adult without constantly trying to change your mother's quirky attitude. Keep in mind that if you repeatedly and too zealously strive to gain your mother's respect, she is likely to view such strivings as a sign of your immaturity and might as a result feel empowered to further demean you.

Q: I like a guy and have his phone number. I want to call him and ask him to go somewhere with me, but I don't know how to begin.

A: Many people feel the jitters when they take the risk of asking someone they only slightly know for a date. Sometimes a person's anxieties over meeting such challenges will grow and fester with the passage of time. Therefore, it is probably a good idea to make your call as soon as it's convenient, before this emotional mole-hill becomes a Himalayan mountain.

It might also be advisable to plan beforehand how you might wish to spend your prospective date with this guy. Then assuming he consents to the date, you will be better prepared with helpful suggestions for your first outing together. Naturally, give him a chance to suggest a time and place as well. If your voice quavers a bit over the phone and you can't remember your own name, don't let this discourage or defeat you. He'll probably understand. If he doesn't, he may not be worth dating.

Q: I have a crush on my teacher and I don't know if I should do anything about it. We're in college, aren't we, but I'm concerned about our age difference and gossip, among other things. I think my teacher has the same feelings toward me. What should I do?

A: Social and romantic relationships between students and instructors can be a sticky business. For example, personal relationships with students may cause some instructors to lose their professional objectivity (and at some schools, their jobs). As a result, their affections may influence how they academically evaluate their student heartthrobs. Also, as you have mentioned, personal relationships between students and instructors are often detected by classmates. Nasty gossip may ensue.

If you really can't bank your fires for this instructor and are willing to expose yourself to many potential hazards, it might be helpful to privately ask your instructor if he or she truly reciprocates your feelings. Don't be shocked, however, if you are told that your instructor's interest in you is strictly of an academic nature.

Q: How do I deal with a cross-cultural relationship when the other person doesn't want to deal with my culture?

A: Assuming that you take pride in your own culture, your partner's chilly attitude will no doubt be damaging to your relationship and to your self-esteem. Is your partner's refusal to "deal with" your culture a sign of bigotry or just plain ignorance, or perhaps both? In either case, you may sometimes enable other persons to overcome their cultural biases by sharing what you know and value about your own culture with them.

If this doesn't work, you can probably assume that your mate is a close-minded nincompoop and it is time to evaluate whether the relationship is worth sustaining. By all means, don't forfeit your pride in your cultural heritage in order to win over and please others. That type of thinking usually leads to trouble.

Q: A friend of mine is very shy and lacks self-confidence. I try to help her by giving her compliments and encouraging her to do more things with her life, but she always finds some excuse to rebuff my efforts. What steps should she or I take toward getting her to realize her self-worth?

A: Your concern for your shy friend is obviously genuine and commendable. However, in your zeal to be a good buddy you may be overlooking some of the psychological obstacles and complexities that arise in assisting persons who suffer from low self-esteem. One's sense of self-esteem develops most profoundly during childhood. To oversimplify matters quite a bit, when a child receives appreciation, respect and affirmation within her family, she ordinarily will come to value herself with confidence and self-respect. However, where there is considerable disrespect, devaluation and contempt for the child, that child will most likely grow up with a shaky sense of self, a good degree of social shyness and a certain lack of initiative.

When you generously compliment your friend, this flattery tends to clash with her low self-concept. This clash, unfortunately, does not necessarily raise her self-esteem. Since she already lacks a sense of self-worth, her reaction to your compliments may be as follows: She may feel that you are patronizing and deceiving her since she "knows" in her heart that she is worthless and, therefore, you must either be mistaken and naïve about her true personal value or you are lying to her in order to curry favor with her.

To possibly make matters worse, she may appreciate your heartfelt attempts to bolster her ego, but she might feel even more disappointed in herself as a result of your efforts since she evidently can't satisfactorily fulfill your wishes and expectations that she improve herself. In other words, your intense desire and efforts to help your friend find her real worth may, paradoxically, actually serve to lower her self-esteem if she feels that she keeps disappointing you.

I would suggest that you for the time being strive to accept rather than change your friend's shyness and social limitations, however painful or frustrating that may be for you. Respecting our friends' inability to be the kind of people we would prefer them to be is an excellent way of showing our appreciation for them. Quite often, accepting other persons just as they are, psychological blemishes and all, provides them with exactly the inspiration they need to change and grow. Try this tactful approach and, above all, be patient.

Q: Can you please explain the term "anal retentive?" I've heard it being used a lot in conversations lately and have a vague idea of its meeting, but I was wondering if you could possibly elaborate on this.

A: It is indeed curious that the term anal retentive is receiving so much currency in our everyday conversations. Apparently, most people who use the term don't realize that the concept of the anal retentive personality was originated by Sigmund Freud a great many years ago.

Freud postulated that overly harsh or coercive toilet training caused the young child first to feel powerless and then, in order to compensate for this state of powerlessness, to assert itself by tightening its sphincters. The child thus deals with superior forces (the pressuring parents) by refusing to defecate. Gradually, he learns that he can control and thwart his parents by being stubborn and retentive in this manner. If the pattern is not somehow altered, the child acquires the belief that stubbornness and retentiveness are desirable traits, so it will adopt these characteristics as a general means of mastering problems and dealing with life.

The main traits of the anal retentive character are orderliness, extreme frugality and obstinacy. Such a person's obstinacy may become so extreme that he may feel compelled to always do the exact opposite of what is required. This obstinacy might be viewed as the passive expression of those resentments and sadistic thoughts that were first aroused when, as a child, he was being pressured to "produce" on the potty.

Psychoanalysts have also suggested that the anal retentive character treats money as he had originally treated his own feces; that is, by holding on to it, rigidly and fanatically.

Obviously, the term anal retentive is very unflattering and should be used, like the kindred term "asshole," only for the purpose of insulting another person. It is also curious how often the term asshole creeps into everyday conversation, isn't it? This term, which, as far as I know, was not coined by Sigmund Freud, applies to the person who metaphorically dumps his feces onto others, usually in the form of anger, disrespect and sadism. I must confess that I know nothing about the early toilet training of the character known as the asshole. In any case, the extent to which these two excretory terms have entered into common usage in our social language causes me to suspect that we are rapidly becoming a race of raging coprophiliacs. Anyone who does not agree with me is obviously an anal retentive character.

Q: I've found that I'm totally obsessed with my cat. My mother thinks I'm ready for children and my boyfriend is feeling neglected. I try to defend myself, and they keep insinuating that this is abnormal behavior. Should I be concerned?

A: I'm really not sure what you mean by the word "obsessed" when you describe your feelings toward your cat. Obviously, many people develop profound emotional attachments toward their pets that are both healthy and fulfilling. If, however, your preoccupations with your cat are beginning to replace or interfere with the human relationships in your life, this might indicate the beginning of a problem.

Many people relish the exclusive company of pets because they wish or need to avoid dealing with the ordinary bumps and complications that arise in human relationships. Pets are generally docile. They unconditionally appreciate and reciprocate affection and love, and they don't contradict or ridicule our most absurd and irrational ideas or opinions. They are usually readily available when we need them, and almost never abandon us until they die. They don't care how we look and never judge our personal shortcomings. Pets welcome us home with the fanfare of a slobbery kiss or grand meow and they almost always easily forgive our occasional acts of meanness.

Good human beings have many of these same qualities but they usually don't exhibit them quite so consistently and unconditionally as do some animals. Those people who find it especially difficult to accept this fact may then immerse themselves in exclusive relationships with their pets. In short, if you think that your attachment to your feline friend is indeed, as your boyfriend suggests, leading to your estrangement from people who are important to you, it might be time to re-evaluate your reasons for this intense attachment.

Q: Is it true that if you have a messy room, then your life is a mess? Do I have to clean up my house to show people that I'm a "together" person?

A: Neither tidiness nor messiness is in itself a reflection of the state of one's mind. If memory serves me correctly, this point is dramatically illustrated in the wonderful movie, *The Miracle Worker,* which depicts the childhood of Helen Keller. Helen's father, a rather brittle and narrow-minded man with a penchant for order and tidiness, proclaims to Helen's teacher that cleanliness is next to godliness. Helen's teacher, a woman of profound intelligence and sensitivity, dismisses this cliché by replying, "Cleanliness is next to nothing."

Apropos of this subject, I recall reading about a distinguished contemporary novelist, a Nobel laureate, whose home was continually cluttered with miscellaneous manuscripts and books. Obviously, the chaos in this novelist's household hardly reflected or stemmed from a disordered mind.

At the risk of appearing to contradict myself, I should point out that it is true that some persons who experience depression lose the energy and inclination to clean up their immediate surroundings. A vicious cycle can ensue when the messy surroundings themselves begin to engender even deeper feelings of futility and despair.

In such circumstances, the mess comes to represent to the depressed person a daily reminder of the depression itself, thereby making it all the harder to tackle a good cleanup. A person who is faced with such a dilemma may find it advisable to temporarily put aside some negative emotions in order to attack the clutter as if one were dealing with a malevolent adversary.

As for you, if you prefer a messy house, I suggest you keep it that way. However, if your housekeeping standards begin to erode your friends' willingness to visit you, you might need to reconsider the wisdom of your current lifestyle.

Q: Why is marriage such a scary question for my boyfriend and me? We can't seem to get up the gumption to tie the knot. We are living together now and it seems silly to restrict ourselves simply because there are no rings on our fingers.

A: Although some people regard marriage as only a mere social convention or ritual, this ancient institution still holds a very special significance for a great many others. For some, the transition from simply "living together" to "tying the knot" in matrimony represents a solemnization of the relationship. Marriage, for these individuals, implies a solemn commitment to one another and the assumption of deeper and more long-term vows to fulfill personal responsibilities in behalf of a loved one.

For some couples celibacy permits the postponement of decisions regarding the prospect of having children. Legal matrimony seems to increase the pressure to deal with decisions about the advisability of raising children.

It appears that the postponement or avoidance of marriage also provides some couples with a reassuring sense of freedom. As they perceive matters, as long as they are not legally bonded in matrimony, they can, if their relationship somehow sours, escape from one another with relative ease. The fact that a legal marriage is somewhat more difficult to dissolve and abandon may cause them to feel that marriage is a form of suffocating entrapment that must be avoided at all costs.

Finally, many persons who have grown up with parents who have divorced or had miserable marriages develop a distrustful attitude toward marriage as an institution. They see their parents' failed marriages as proof that marriages in general do not succeed. As a result, they develop fears that, should they themselves take this fateful step, their own marriage would be destined to fail. Since about half of all marriages actually end in divorce, there may be, from a purely statistical standpoint, few objective reasons to believe that their worst fears will not come true.

Q: Since childhood I have had a tendency to do well in my studies for a short while and then to suddenly and mysteriously lose interest in my work and either fail my courses or drop out. I know I am bright, but I can't seem to break this pattern. What's going on and what can I do about it?

A: I have met many students who have had this difficulty. In exploring the early origins of their long-standing inability to sustain their drive to succeed academically, some interesting facts often come to the fore. It seems that many of these students have grown up with parents who are quite fanatical and punitive in dealing with their child's academic pursuits. Some of these parents hover over their children and menacingly criticize their occasional lapses and mistakes. They tend to chastise and humiliate the child who brings home a bad report card, for example. When the child receives a preponderance of excellent grades, however, the parents tend to ignore this positive achievement and magnify the importance of the occasional poor grade.

In time, the child justifiably perceives that his parents' interest in his studies and academic success is quite self-centered. He realizes that his parents are more interested in the end result of his studies—good grades, a diploma from a respectable educational institution and ultimate financial success—than in what and how he actually learns from his scholarly pursuits. He also may draw the warranted conclusion that his parents are more concerned with how his academic success will ultimately reflect upon them than with the level of true personal fulfillment he may eventually derive from his studies. When he gradually discovers that his parents are not genuinely interested in the quality of his academic experience, he often suffers disappointment and a resultant loss of inspiration. What happens next?

Well, over a period of time (many years, in some cases), the student acquires a conscious knowledge that academic achievement is definitely in his own interest and is an intrinsically worthwhile goal. However, if he still has unresolved feelings of anger toward his parents for the way they undermined his earlier attempts to study and learn, he may then harbor the unconscious wish to inflict disappointment and pain upon them through an act of retaliation. In his vengeful mind, the retaliation takes the form of a largely unconscious belief that if he fails academically, his parents will suffer emotional pain.

Now the student is impaled on the horns of his own painful dilemma. He has two conflicting incentives. One is a conscious wish to succeed academically for himself and the second is a largely unconscious need to fail academically in order to triumph over and defeat the egotistical demands of his parents. How does he go about resolving or at least acting out this particular conflict?

Well, at first he is able to perform well on the basis of his conscious and healthy desire to be academically successful. For the time being, he is able to keep his own personal interests in the forefront of his ambitions. However, without quite knowing why, he suddenly discovers that the academic headway he has made is causing him anxiety and depression. Without realizing that he has unconsciously encountered his ongoing conflict with his parents, he is suddenly faced with the fact that if he continues to succeed academically, he will not be able to fulfill his long-harbored wish to see his parents suffer as a result of his failure. In the end, he may, unfortunately, yield to the power of this vindictive fantasy by simply losing interest in his studies and giving up, compelled by unconscious forces to resume the frustrating process in the following semester.

Of course, I do not know if the above-described scenario applies to you, but I have seen a great many students who have struggled with this particular problem due to such conflicts with their parents. One such student is described in the clinical vignette entitled "The 'Fuck You' Alarm Clock" that appears as a chapter in my book *The Mystified Fortune-Teller and Other Tales from Psychotherapy*. As you can see, the problem is a rather complicated one and, for this reason, its resolution sometimes requires psychotherapy. Please keep in mind, I said complicated, not impossible. Many students with chronic academic difficulties gradually acquire a sense of motivation and inspiration after they finally identify and resolve the emotional conflicts that have blocked their way.

Q: I have a friend who shoplifts. She hasn't been caught yet, but I'm worried about her. She doesn't really need or use some of the things she steals and, considering her decent income, she could easily afford to buy the items herself. What's this about?

A: When a person has a compulsion to steal (sometimes referred to as kleptomania) that is not based upon economic circumstances or necessity, it is generally caused by an underlying, largely unconscious, psychological conflict. Such persons have often been denied, or believe they have been denied, sufficient supplies of love, affection and nurturance during their childhood years.

As a result, they develop intense and relentless feelings of vengefulness. In their unending quest for parental love, persons with kleptomaniac tendencies come to regard stolen material objects (such as a dress or wallet) as substitutes or compensations for the affection they allegedly did not receive as children. In other words, the stores from which such persons steal are symbolically viewed as sources of parental emotional "goodies" which, since they supposedly had never been willingly and freely given in the first place, must now be stolen. To put the unconscious formula into words: "If you don't give it to me, I'll take it."

The reckless abandon with which some persons shoplift suggests other dynamics as well. First, the recklessness may suggest that some kleptomaniacs, although bent on revenge, may also feel guilty about their antisocial behavior and are acting heedlessly in order to get caught and punished. The punishment, in effect, would serve not only as an unconscious atonement for their current crimes but, additionally, for their original, symbolic "crime" of seeking love from sources that would not or could not fulfill their deepest emotional needs when they were children.

Second, the kleptomaniac's indiscriminate and dangerous behavior may also represent, at bottom, a plea for help. Because the use of direct appeals for emotional support are viewed by the kleptomaniac with suspicion and fear, due most likely to earlier experiences of acute emotional rejection, the current plea for help must be expressed in an indirect and disguised form—stealing. As sometimes happens, the kleptomaniac is caught, prosecuted and referred for psychological counseling. Thus, the need for help is finally acknowledged and, hopefully, treated and resolved.

Let's hope your friend gets the psychological help she needs before she gets herself into legal difficulties. As a trusted friend, you might inform her that psychotherapy can be quite helpful in remedying problems of compulsive stealing.

Q: My father and I both suffer from a bad temper whenever either of us feels we have been wronged. How much of one's temper is hereditary and how much is learned?

A: Studies of newborns suggest that some individuals are genetically disposed to being more active and excitable than others. However, the development of a truly "bad" temper is more than likely predominantly based upon one's emotional experiences as a child, primarily in relation to those with whom the child most closely identified—parents, siblings, grandparents, teachers, etc.

You have mentioned that you and your father become especially riled whenever you feel that you have been wronged. This suggests that during your formative years you probably strongly identified with two characteristics of his personality (as well as a great many others, no doubt). The first is his tendency to magnify both the seriousness of the personal injustices and slights he has encountered and the extent to which he has been truly injured by those perceived injustices. The second is his relative lack of perspective and resiliency in dealing with disappointment and frustration.

Why, you might ask, would a child identify with a personality characteristic of a parent that is socially undesirable and troublesome? Well, partly because most young children, being by nature rather dependent and impressionable, grow up admiring and emulating their parents quite unconditionally, and are therefore not in a position to clearly distinguish between those of their parents' personality characteristics that are wholesome and those that are not. Unfortunately, it is only much later, when they are adults, that many people discover that they have adopted some of the unattractive and undesirable traits of their parents.

A second explanation for this problem is the fact that many undesirable traits of parents, such as a nasty temper, can be quite frightening to a young child. The child, out of fear and helplessness, defends herself against the onslaught by developing the selfsame characteristics as the frightening parent—in this case, a tendency to lose her temper when thwarted. It is often by this psychological process—known by the psychoanalytic school as "identification with the aggressor"—rather than by dint of one's genes, that the personality trait of a bad temper is transmitted from generation to generation.

Q: I have a friend who is very overweight, and I am very thin. I feel self-conscious about my weight, thinking it intimidates her. How do I encourage her to diet? Coming from a thin person, I don't feel it's my right to say anything, but I want to give her some support.

A: I'm reminded by your letter of a joke, a rather bad joke I'm afraid, about two persons, one obese, the other very thin, who used their chance encounter to ridicule one another. The obese person jousted first by remarking to the thin one, "From the looks of you, there has been a terrible famine." The thin one rejoined, "And from the looks of you, you caused it."

Now, to return to your question, I think it is best that you use discretion and patience in assisting your overweight friend. Being extremely overweight is often caused by a genetic predisposition combined with complicated emotional factors that can be aggravated by peer pressure. Your self-consciousness in the company of your friend and your desire to encourage her toward better self-care obviously stem from your feelings of empathy for her. Use this empathy to respect her right and her need to remain overweight until she herself decides to change that aspect of her life.

In the meantime, perhaps as her good friend you can also serve as a good role model from whom she can eventually learn something about how to take better care of herself. In any case, don't, if you can help it, allow your guilt to goad you into attempts to direct her personal affairs. That sort of thing could jeopardize your friendship. Finally, if it is not too uncomfortable for you, you might consider telling her how you feel about the physical differences between you. Such conversations will probably be awkward at first. But, if carried out with mutual respect and sensitivity, they could conceivably deepen your relationship.

Q: I've done a lot of traveling in my life and have developed deep friendships abroad. My problem is that I haven't been able to do the same here. I meet plenty of people but never seem to get to know them and seldom do we do things together. Why is this?

A: It is difficult to know exactly why you are more successful making friends when you are gallivanting abroad than when you are anchored to the environs of your home. Some people act differently when they leave home because they feel liberated by their brief escape from the everyday constraints imposed upon them by family, friends, employers, etc. The accountability and inhibitions they usually display in relation to those people are cast aside as soon as they leave their home base, replaced by a more carefree attitude toward the relatively transient friendships one tends to make while one is traveling. You describe your friendships abroad as "deep." Are they really deep or do they simply appear to be deep because they are intense and exhilarating and *safe* based upon the fact that they are intrinsically and predictably short-term, not allowing for much genuine intimacy? In other words, do your failure to develop deep friendships with people close to home and your success in forming better, albeit short-term, friendships abroad stem from the same source: a limited capacity for genuine intimacy on your part?

When strangers meet on a vacation, ordinarily their only (conscious) expectation is that they will enjoy one another's company to the utmost for the quite finite duration of the relationship. This expectation in itself can induce an openness and spontaneity. This explains why some people disclose their innermost, heretofore hidden, personal secrets to complete strangers on airplanes and at faraway resorts. There's not much personal risk when you know you won't see the confidant again, at least not for a long time. True intimacy usually entails openness and stick-to-itiveness with friends and partners over an appreciable period of time. What is an *appreciable* period of time? I'll let you decide.

If any of my comments seem relevant to your feelings of loneliness and self-doubt, it might be advisable for you to seek personal counseling as a means of resolving your dilemma.

Q: I'm no longer attracted to my husband, but I'm afraid to leave him because of the security he provides. So now I find myself getting involved in extramarital affairs. Should I seek help or is this something that will resolve itself?

A: The fact that you are no longer attracted to your husband obviously has left you feeling bereft and empty. Your attempts to overcome your state of emotional emptiness with the transitory sparks ignited by extramarital affairs are at best only temporarily lifting you out of the doldrums. Evidently, your extramarital affairs represent the desperation, anger and resentment you feel toward your husband because he no longer attracts you.

Rather than frenetically and disappointingly leap-frog from affair to affair, you might attempt to discuss your negative feelings with your husband, directly and honestly. Give your husband a fair chance to respond to your feelings without condemning or censuring him for his shortcomings. If you find that such talks are either too uncomfortable or unproductive, you both might benefit more by availing yourselves of couple counseling.

If you then discover that, despite your best efforts, you are still disgruntled with your husband, but cannot leave him due to the fear of losing the security he provides, you most assuredly should enter individual therapy in order to address and resolve such fears. I would venture to guess that your central difficulty is a fear of abandonment, quite a common fear among individuals who cling to extremely unattractive and unfulfilling relationships.

Q: I have a friend who has been suffering from alcohol and drug abuse. I got her into an excellent rehab center and have even been going to some AA meetings with her. Everyone keeps warning me of "co-dependency." At the risk of sounding naïve, I haven't let on that I don't truly know what that term means. Can you shed some light on this subject for me?

A: The by-now overused term "co-dependency" usually refers to a person's tendency to collude with and contribute to another person's bad habits or addictions. For many individuals, co-dependency is carried out on an unconscious level.

For example, a woman may consciously, sincerely and deeply desire that her husband overcome his chronic self-abuse with drugs and alcohol. Yet, by providing her husband with many years of unstintingly patient support and understanding, she has, in his eyes, given him a sense of license to continue behaving self-destructively. Often, co-dependent persons are overly tolerant, wishy-washy and inordinately forgiving. They are prone to feeling guilty and remorseful whenever they assert their own rights and needs. Therefore, their partners easily manipulate and steamroll over them. Typical addicts and alcoholics use denial as a defense mechanism to refute the fact that they are indeed addictive personalities. Interestingly enough, co-dependent persons also use denial to blind themselves to the severity and destructiveness of their partners' addictions.

If your friends are warning you about co-dependency, it is possible that you are over-invested in curing your alcoholic friend's problems. If so, you might find psychological counseling for yourself to be an eye-opener.

Q: My father insists on involving himself in my educational affairs. He's pushy about the kind of courses I should take, and in what area I should major. From past experiences, while in high school, I felt his involvement was not very helpful. Now that I'm an adult, I'd like to make my own decisions. How can I explain this to him without offending him?

A: Many parents over-involve themselves in the academic and career pursuits of their children. As a result, despite the best of intentions, their advice and guidance are often untimely and unwarranted. It sounds like your father, considering his intense emotional investment in your schoolwork, is viewing your academic success as a symbol of his own self-worth. In other words, he regards your academic attainments as a feather in his own parental cap. Although self-centered pride of this kind is not always destructive, it seems that your father has carried his campaign in behalf of your educational success much too far.

I would suggest that you explain to your father that you appreciate his assistance, but that it is essential to your personal welfare that you determine and fulfill your own educational objectives. It might be especially helpful to remind him of two central points: (a) ultimate personal happiness in one's chosen academic and professional career usually evolves from studying and mastering subject areas that uniquely suit one's own, not someone else's, interests and aptitudes; (b) that you fully expect your academic choices to be fraught with mistakes and problems. However, experimentally making and learning from unavoidable mistakes is an intrinsic part of one's educational experience and therefore should not be criticized, censured or discouraged.

Finally, if after having had this heart-to-heart talk with your father, he is still as unreasonable and unconvinced as ever, it may be time to realize that there is little you can do at this time to avoid offending him by your assertion of academic independence. That might be the price you will have to pay for attaining the goals to which you aspire.

Q: Over the years there has been a great deal of news coverage regarding the problem of acquaintance rape. Could you shed some light on this problem?

A: The problem of acquaintance or date rape on the contemporary college campuses of this country is very widespread and extremely serious. In one survey of women on 32 college campuses, 15 percent had experienced at least one rape, and 89 percent of the time the rapes were committed by men the women knew. Three-quarters of the victims in this study did not identify their experience as rape and none of the males involved believed they had committed a crime. About 45 percent of the males who committed acquaintance rape said they would repeat the experience. More than one-third of the rape victims did not discuss the experience with anyone and more than 90 percent of them did not report the incident to the police. As a result, relatively few date rapes are ever prosecuted and even fewer lead to the conviction of the assailant.

In another study, when men were asked if there was any likelihood they would force a woman to have sex against her will if they could get away with it, about half said they would. But when the same men were asked if they would *rape* a woman if they knew they could get away with it, only about 15 percent said they would. Evidently, many men don't realize that forcing a woman to have sex against her will is rape.

The American College Health Association has recommended the following ways to reduce the risk of rape.

For women:

1. Believe in your right to set limits. Say "No" when you mean "No."
2. Be assertive with someone who is sexually pressuring you. Passivity may be interpreted as permission.
3. Remember that some men assume that sexy dress wear and a flirtatious manner mean a desire for sex.
4. Pay attention to what is happening around you. Don't put yourself in vulnerable positions.
5. Avoid the overuse of drugs or alcohol.

For men:

1. Be aware of social pressures. It's okay not to "score."
2. "No" means "No." Don't continue after "No."
3. Don't assume that sexy dress wear and a flirtatious manner are invitations to have sex.
4. Avoid the excessive use of drugs and alcohol.

An excellent book on this subject is *Real Rape* by Susan Estrich, a law professor who was herself a rape victim.

Q: My new girlfriend has a son who's almost three. Sometimes when I'm visiting her house the boy will approach me, push at the fly of my pants and ask me, "What's that?" This is somewhat unnerving to me. My girlfriend says I should just tell him that it's my "pee-pee" and then ignore further prodding from him on the subject—I suppose she means physically or verbally speaking. I have reason to suspect that her son may also have seen his mother and me making love. As I'm an only child and have limited experience with kids, could you advise me on how to broach intimate subjects and bodily functions with this child?

A: Ordinarily, it is advisable to discuss sex with children in a calm and factual manner. By factual, I of course do not mean that you should launch into a heavy and long scientific discussion about the human plumbing and reproductive systems. If your girlfriend's son unnerves you with his sexual curiosity, it may be necessary to tell him that, although you are a bit shy and uncomfortable with the subject, you will nevertheless do the best you can to answer his questions. This approach may enable him to realize that when his questions make you nervous it is not his fault.

You naturally have the prerogative, which I think you should exercise, to tell him with some firmness and repetition you prefer that he not touch your genitals. If done without punitive severity, this can be an effective means of conveying your wish to have your own bodily integrity treated with respect. It is especially important for young children to understand this principle of respect since how they will ultimately treat their own bodies and the bodies of their future loved ones will probably depend upon such understanding.

I think you are asking for trouble by exposing the child to your lovemaking with his mother. Such experiences for children usually lead to feelings of intense helplessness, jealousy and a wide variety of behavioral problems. So, keep the door shut and make sure the boy is safely ensconced in his own bed before you go at it.

By the way, there is an excellent book, written many years ago, called *Where Do Babies Come From?*, which answers the sexual questions of children with remarkable wit, wisdom and factuality. I suggest that you read this delightful book to your girlfriend's son. I think you'll both enjoy it immensely and, as a bonus, the experience of reading it to him might even melt some of your nervousness about broaching intimate subjects with the boy. Incidentally, if you want to use the term "pee-pee," that's okay, but, to paraphrase Gertrude Stein, a penis is a penis is a penis.

Q: I have a new boyfriend. We have a lot of the same interests, in movies, music, etc. But it seems that whenever we talk about something serious, like politics or religion, we fight. Is this normal?

A: Jonathan Swift wrote, "We have just enough religion to make us hate, but not enough to make us love one another." As for the subject of politics, Will Rogers said, "I tell you folks, all politics is applesauce."

For most people, the subjects of politics and religion are suffused with highly important personal values and aspirations. Practically all of the essential ideals that have guided our lives since early childhood can find expression in our political and religious convictions and affiliations. Therefore, when someone questions or assails our religious or political beliefs, we commonly react by feeling that an attack has been made upon our deepest values and ideals. Frequently, we even react by feeling, at least on the unconscious level, that someone who questions our political and religious beliefs is really debasing our families and our very selves. This is why discussions that deal with the topics of religion and politics can become so heated and nasty.

In any case, it sounds like the feuds you are having with your boyfriend are fairly normal and perhaps can even be intellectually stimulating and enriching for the two of you. If, however, your political arguments with your boyfriend eventually reach the level of vicious mud-slinging and obfuscation that characterizes many of the debates between political candidates in this country, then your relationship is definitely in serious trouble and you should seek counseling immediately.

Q: I am the manager of an apartment house in which a good friend of mine resides. My friend suffers from a mental illness that periodically causes her to lose control of her emotions, cry and scream hysterically and seriously disturb the peace and quiet of my tenants. I want to help her (she does already receive psychiatric treatment, at times as an in-patient), but I also have a responsibility to my tenants. How I can resolve this problem?

A: The way to resolve a problem such as you've described is very similar to how porcupines make love: with a good degree of difficulty and some pain. It is apparent that there is little you can do to prevent or curtail your friend's periodic emotional outbursts. If psychiatric treatment and multiple hospitalizations have not done the trick, it is not likely that your help, no matter how well intentioned, will have much of an overall impact upon her condition. In your role as her friend, it may therefore simply be necessary to accept and tolerate your friend's mental illness as a disability over which she has little control and for which she requires much compassion.

As for the matter of your other role as manager of the apartment house in which your friend lives, you may have responsibilities to the other tenants that sometimes conflict with or supersede your responsibilities to your friend. For example, some tenants, out of exasperation over your friend's disturbing behavior, may demand that you have her evicted or arrested and, if you don't comply, they may complain to your employer, thus jeopardizing your job. If matters reach such serious proportions, you might be faced with the unpalatable choice of losing your tenants and your job or losing a friendship. Loss of one's livelihood is of course a heavy price to pay for the preservation of a friendship, but only you can decide whether such a sacrifice is merited.

It is possible, of course, that your friend might be amenable to living in the protective care of a halfway house where other patients, psychiatrically disabled people like herself, would be more readily tolerated and assisted than would ever be possible in the apartment house. You might suggest this idea to her and see if she might be willing to allow you to help her expedite it.

One other, perhaps unrealistic, idea occurs to me. Perhaps you could candidly speak to each of the complaining tenants about your friend's psychiatric disability. You could explain that her outbursts are uncontrollable symptoms of an illness that are not in themselves dangerous, last for only brief periods and are responsibly attended to by local psychiatric agencies. These explanations might allay some of the worry and fear aroused by your friend's disturbing behavior and eventually lead to a more tolerant attitude toward her. To pursue this course of action will naturally require much time and patience on your part, a sacrifice the merits of which only you can determine.

Q: My boyfriend and I generally get along quite well. Once in a while, however, his temper flares up and he hits me. I've warned him many times that I would leave him if he did it again, but he continues to hit me even after firmly promising that he would not. Now he tells me that he'd like to marry me and that being married to me would cure him of his violent temper and physical abusiveness. The thought tempts me, but I'm afraid. What do you think?

A: Your question is a no-brainer. I think you should be afraid, very afraid. Your boyfriend is either deluding himself or is lying to you. Marriage per se is a cure for nothing but celibacy. Usually, men who beat women do so because of a serious flaw in their character. Such men generally have grown up in families where violence is commonplace. Quite often, their fathers have beaten their mothers with regularity and impunity. The violence of the father and the excessive passivity of the mother who tolerates spousal abuse are observed by the child with a sense of rage and helplessness.

The child who grows up in such a family environment may develop a number of pathological attitudes that evolve from his feelings of rage and helplessness. First, although he may hate and resent his father's violence toward his mother, he may also, after watching how much his father got away with abusive behavior, develop his own attitude that a man's physical or economic power to intimidate women gives him a broad license to mistreat them. From watching his mother passively absorb and tolerate abuse day after day he may also develop the erroneous belief that women are nothing more than defenseless and contemptible objects that deserve to be abusively treated.

To suggest that your boyfriend will attain a cure for his abusiveness through matrimony is to indulge in dangerous daydreaming and magical illusion. Because such destructive attitudes are usually deeply embedded in the personality quite early in life, they are ordinarily quite difficult to eliminate or even reduce in the inveterate abuser of women. The person (such as your boyfriend) who exhibits such attitudes and behavior needs professional psychological help. The first positive step he could take would be to admit that he has a serious problem and then do something constructive about it by entering therapy. However, if you do suggest to him that he seek professional help don't be surprised if he comes up with 12,478 reasons why this is a bad idea because he's going to miraculously and completely reform himself tomorrow, entirely on his own and solely by dint of his prodigious will power.

Q: I am suffering stress due to an extremely tight schedule. I work full-time at night and carry twelve units of classes during the day. I never seem to have enough time to study with any degree of continuity and it's showing in my grades. Grades are important, but so are paying the bills and eating.

To compound this problem, I worry about this predicament constantly. I can't get the sleep I need (not that my schedule allows this luxury in the first place). I have read time-management books, but they don't seem to offer realistic solutions. What can I do to relieve this stress?

A: Unfortunately, there are large numbers of students who simultaneously undertake excessive academic and vocational loads that eventually become physically and emotionally overtaxing. All too often, unless one is somehow blessed with extraordinary energy and resilience, carrying the weight of a full-time job, as well as a full-time academic schedule, can be an excruciating predicament.

Considering the fact that you are already suffering from a falloff in the quality of your academic work and sleep has become a scarce commodity, this probably is an opportune time to re-evaluate the wisdom of your original choice to impose such Herculean demands upon yourself. If I may hazard a few guesses, I think you have probably overestimated yourself in thinking that you could tackle this superhuman feat without suffering serious consequences. If you are like many other students who struggle with such predicaments, you probably believed that you could effectively shorten your college career and more quickly find gainful employment in your chosen field by maintaining a hefty academic schedule regardless of the awful toll it might take upon your physical and mental health.

If, for financial reasons, you cannot curtail your work schedule, you should give serious consideration to pruning down your course load. At first, this thought may disappoint and discourage you and even cause you to feel like a failure. Try to realize, however, that this experience does not truly represent a personal failure on your part; but rather, it merely reflects your inability to cope with an inordinately difficult set of physical and emotional demands.

Finally, keep in mind that it is ordinarily much better to delay the attainment of cherished goals in order to safeguard one's physical and mental health than to stay on an accelerated treadmill that can end in serious illness and further disappointment.